WHO WE ARE

WHO WE ARE

A SNAPSHOT OF AUSTRALIA TODAY

DAVID DALE

ALLEN&UNWIN

First published in hardback 2006

Paperback edition first updated and published 2007

Allen & Unwin
83 Alexander Street
Crows Nest NSW 2065
Australia

Phone: (61 2) 8425 0100
Fax: (61 2) 9906 2218
Email: info@allenandunwin.com
Web: www.allenandunwin.com

National Library of Australia
Cataloguing-in-Publication entry:

Dale, David, 1948–

  Who we are: a snapshot of Australia today.
  Includes index.

  ISBN 978 1 74175 087 4
  ISBN 1 74175 087 3

  1. National characteristics, Australian. 2. Australia –
  Social life and customs. 3. Australia – Economic
  conditions. 4. Australia – History. I. Title.

306.0994

Internal design and typesetting by Steven Dunbar
Printed by McPhersons Printing Group, Australia

10 9 8 7 6 5 4 3 2 1

CONTENTS

INTRODUCTION

Every so often a politician or pundit goes on about what 'the average Australian' wants, believes, expects and won't stand for. Every so often a pundit or politician discovers the importance of teaching 'Australian values' to recent arrivals or describes some action or group as 'un-Australian'. These propositions are usually followed by a flurry of questions, and the revelation that the pundits and politicians have no idea what they're talking about.

We're here to help. This book is an attempt to provide all the information anybody could need to determine what it means to be a resident of this continent, what might be our national values and whether there is — or ever could be — an average, normal or typical way of living here. In particular, this book tries to explain how, in just fifty years, this country transformed itself from one of the dullest places on the planet to one of the most interesting.

You can tell a lot about a nation from the way it shops, talks, eats, laughs, worships, competes and entertains itself. That's the kind of detail you'll find in this book — our favourite movies, our political passions, our inventions, our most popular products, our world records, our changing language and, above all, the kind of people we celebrate and satirise. There's a bit of history here but this is mainly about the way we are in the first decade of the 21st century — a reality that may be somewhat different from the myths Australians hold about their land.

You'll find mention of lamingtons, Holden cars, Don Bradman, echidnas, Slim Dusty, funnel-webs and *The Man from Snowy River*. But you'll also find tiramisu, 'Desperate Housewives', chardonnay, Bob Brown, iPods, Nicole Kidman and 'Beds are Burning' — which may be more relevant to the national identity in 2007.

One of our healthiest national traits is a habit of making fun of ourselves. Australians are uncomfortable with displays of patriotism. They'd rather trim tall poppies than boast about triumphs. So when I say there are a few things in this book that made me feel surprised and proud as I was researching them, please don't spread it around.

We know we're good at sport and good at acting, but I don't think we've ever seen ourselves as a nation of visionary idealists. Yet you can't help getting that impression when you read the inspiring speeches in chapter 4 and the sections on Stirrers, Investigators, Helpers and Pioneers in chapter 6. And if you look at the Firsts in chapter 3, you suspect there may be a national aptitude for inventing creative solutions to practical problems.

But any heart swellings this book may stir are incidental to its primary purpose, which is to be a reference guide and settler of bets for every modern Australian home. If you don't find the insights you need in the Index, let me know (ddale@essentialideas.info) and I'll try to include them in the next edition.

Many people and institutions helped my research. The Australian Bureau of Statistics (ABS) was my primary source of data, but I also learned much from ACNielsen, the Motion Picture Distributors Association of Australia, OzTAM, the Australian Record Industry Association, GTK Marketing, the Australian Publishers Association and the Audit Bureau of Circulations. My reference works included *The Macquarie Encyclopedia of Australian Events* (Macquarie Library), *2006 Fact Finder* (Hardie Grant), *Measures of Social Progress* (ABS), *Well May We Say … The Speeches That Made Australia* (Black Inc), *The Dinkum Dictionary* by Susan Butler (Text Publishing) and *Stirring Australian Speeches* (Melbourne University Press).

I also need to thank the readers of the *Sydney Morning Herald*, whose thoughtful responses to my weekly column, The Tribal Mind, spurred me on to new inquiries and corrected many a misapprehension.

At Allen & Unwin, I'm grateful to Patrick Gallagher for giving me the idea and Jeanmarie Morosin and Joanne Holliman for putting it into practice. The page designer and mapmaker was Steven Dunbar and the cover was the work of Lisa White. My banderilleros Susan Anthony, Tony Dorigo, Lucio Galletto, Hugh Mackay and Katherine Thomson raised issues I needed to explain. And my wife Susan and daughter Millie offered patience and encouragement beyond the call of duty.

DAVID DALE
September 2006

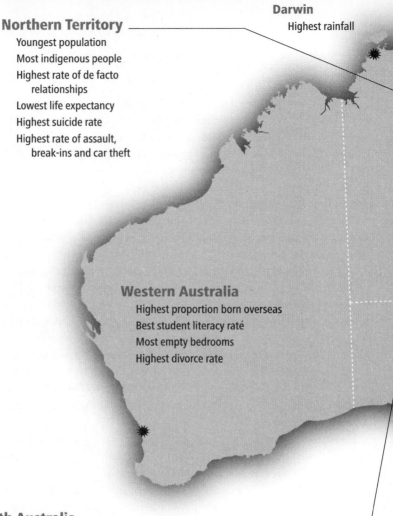

Darwin
Highest rainfall

Northern Territory
Youngest population
Most indigenous people
Highest rate of de facto
    relationships
Lowest life expectancy
Highest suicide rate
Highest rate of assault,
    break-ins and car theft

Western Australia
Highest proportion born overseas
Best student literacy rate
Most empty bedrooms
Highest divorce rate

South Australia
Highest asthma rate
Highest home ownership rate
Most lone-person households

Victoria
Lowest birth rate
Highest drug-induced death rate
Highest car ownership rate

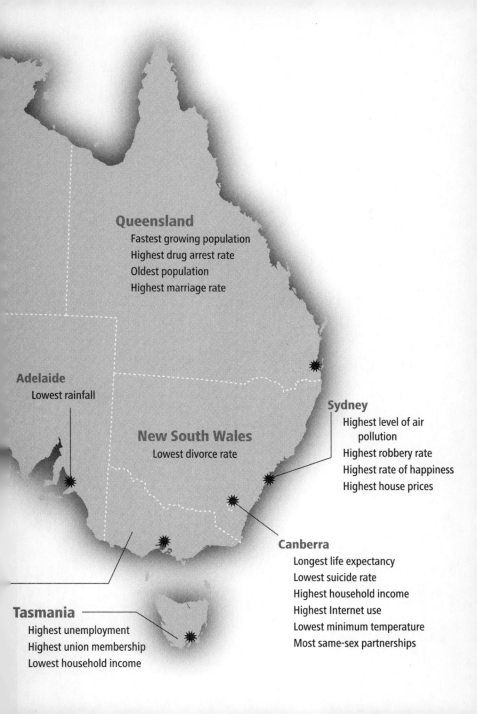

Queensland
  Fastest growing population
  Highest drug arrest rate
  Oldest population
  Highest marriage rate

Adelaide
  Lowest rainfall

New South Wales
  Lowest divorce rate

Sydney
  Highest level of air
    pollution
  Highest robbery rate
  Highest rate of happiness
  Highest house prices

Canberra
  Longest life expectancy
  Lowest suicide rate
  Highest household income
  Highest Internet use
  Lowest minimum temperature
  Most same-sex partnerships

Tasmania
  Highest unemployment
  Highest union membership
  Lowest household income

1

THE BITS THAT
MAKE US

First glance

Born in Australia: 76 per cent of the population
Aboriginal: 2.5 per cent
Born in Britain: 6 per cent
Born in New Zealand: 4 per cent
Born in China or Vietnam: 3 per cent
Born in Italy or Greece: 2 per cent
Born in the Middle East: 0.7 per cent
Speaking a language other than English at home: 16 per cent

Catholic: 27 per cent
Anglican: 21 per cent
Buddhist: 1.9 per cent
Muslim: 1.5 per cent
Hindu: 0.5 per cent
Jewish: 0.4 per cent
No religion: 16 per cent

Aged over 37: 50 per cent
In a partnership, with children under 16: 38 per cent
Living alone: 9 per cent
Living within fifty kilometres of the sea: 85 per cent
Living on a farm: 1 per cent
Owning or paying off a home: 70 per cent
Living in a home with three or more bedrooms: 75 per cent
**Proportion of three bedroom homes containing one or
    two people:** 58 per cent
Homeless: 0.5 per cent
Likely to cohabit before marriage: 74 per cent of couples
Likely to get divorced: 43 per cent of marriages

Having a beyond-school qualification (degree, diploma etc.): 51 per cent of adults

Income of less than $600 a week after tax: 50 per cent of adults

Donating to charity more than once a year: 87 per cent of adults (average $424 per Australian household)

Smokers: 21 per cent of adults

Use marijuana: 11 per cent

Use ecstasy: 3 per cent

Drink alcohol at health-risk level: 13 per cent

Classified as overweight or obese: 48 per cent

Feeling in good or excellent health: 82 per cent

With a disability requiring help at home: 11 per cent

Experienced a mental disorder (depression, anxiety) in the past year: 18 per cent

Feel safe at home after dark: 82 per cent

Likely to be the victim of a personal crime this year: 6 per cent

At least one mobile phone : 90 per cent of households

Regular cinema-goers: 72 per cent

In a home with two or more TV sets: 70 per cent

Owning a DVD player: 70 per cent

Using the Internet at least once a week: 60 per cent

Subscribing to pay TV: 25 per cent of households

How many of us

As of 1 December 2006, the **population** of Australia was 20 670 000. According to the Australian Bureau of Statistics (ABS), this figure rises by one person every 2 minutes and 8 seconds. On average, there is a birth every 2 minutes and 4 seconds, a death every 3 minutes and 55 seconds, and a net gain of one international immigrant every 4 minutes and 9 seconds.

Our **population growth** of 1 per cent per year is among the lowest in the world: Indonesia is growing by 1.3 per cent a year, Malaysia by 1.9 per cent and Papua New Guinea by 2.2 per cent. Then again, we have the same rate as the United States and we are way ahead of Japan (0.1 per cent a year) and Italy (declining by 0.1 per cent a year).

The Bureau predicts that we **will reach** 21 million in 2008 and 25 million in 2050, then decline in numbers unless we boost immigration and start breeding like bunnies.

Entrepreneurs think we should **aim** to reach 40 million, the tipping point to make us a world economic player. Environmentalists think we're already bloated because the continent's resources can't sustain more than 12 million people. The Bureau says neither of those scenarios can be achieved this century.

If your idea of **fun** is to watch big numbers changing, go to http://www.abs.gov.au and click on 'Australia's population'. There you'll find the Bureau's nifty people clock. It will send you to other sites which reveal that Australia is the 54th most populated country in the world (China is top with 1.32 billion) and has one of the lowest population densities: two people per square kilometre, compared with Singapore at the top with 6389 per square kilometre and Greenland at the bottom with 0.03 per square kilometre.

This year

250 000 people will be **born** in Australia.

448 000 will **arrive**, intending to stay for more than a year.

338 000 will **leave**, intending to stay away for more than a year.

130 000 will **die**: 29 per cent from cancer, 20 per cent from heart disease, and 9 per cent from stroke.

210 000 will get **married**.

110 000 will get **divorced**.

392 000 will **move** from one state to another.

3.3 million will be at **school**.

1.4 million will work in the **retail trade**.

1.1 million will work in **manufacturing**.

370 000 will work in **agriculture**.

6.5 million will **buy and sell shares**.

23 820 will be in **prison**: 22 180 men and 1640 women.

90 000 **abortions** will be performed in hospitals and private clinics.

800 000 **new cars** will be bought: 21 per cent Toyota, 19 per cent Holden, 14 per cent Ford, 7 per cent Nissan, 6 per cent Mitsubishi.

13.4 million vehicles will be **registered**.

14 600 **kilometres**, the equivalent of two return trips from Sydney to Perth, will be covered by the average car.

1730 people will be **killed by cars**.

5.2 million **travellers from overseas**, mainly from New Zealand, Britain, Japan, the US, Korea, China and Singapore, will enter the country, staying, on average, 27 nights.

3.5 million **trips overseas** will be made by Australians, mainly to New Zealand, Britain, the US, China and Fiji.

12 million **credit cards** will be used to spend $164 billion, with an average outstanding debt of $2600 each per month.

82 million **cinema tickets** will be sold.

Comparisons: then and now

Age

In 1901: 35 per cent of the population were under 15; 4 per cent were over 65; the median age was 22

Now: 20 per cent are under 15; 14 per cent are over 65, and the median age is 37

Life expectancy for males

In 1901: A baby boy could expect to live till 55 years of age

1935: life expectancy was 65

1980: 70

Now: 77

The mix

In 1901: 23 per cent of the population were born overseas (in Britain)

1947: 10 per cent were born overseas (in Britain)

Now: 24 per cent are overseas born (mainly in Britain, New Zealand, Italy, China, Vietnam, Greece and 180 other countries) and 25 per cent of people born here have at least one parent born overseas

Main source countries of immigrants (after Britain)

Arriving in 1962: Greece, Italy, Yugoslavia

1972: Lebanon, New Zealand, Yugoslavia

1982: Vietnam, New Zealand, South Africa

1992: New Zealand, China, Vietnam

Now: New Zealand, China, India

The stay-at-homes

In 1976: 21 per cent of 20 to 29 year olds lived with their parents

Now: 30 per cent do

Marriage age

In 1976: The average age for men to marry was 25; for women 22

Now: It's 30 for men; 28 for women

The wedding service

In 1986: 39 per cent of marriages were performed by a civil celebrant

Now: 55 per cent

Birth rate

In 1901: 4 babies were born per woman

1960: 3.5 per woman

1975: 2 per woman

Now: 1.8 babies are born per woman

In 1956: The median age for women giving birth was 23

1976: It was 26

Now: It's 30

In 1976: 40 per cent of 20 to 29 year olds had children

Now: 16 per cent do

Unemployment

In 1956: 1 per cent

1974: 3 per cent

1983: 10 per cent

1988: 7 per cent

Now: 5 per cent

Inflation

In 1956: 6 per cent

1974: 16 per cent

1983: 9 per cent

1988: 8 per cent

Now: 3 per cent

Comparisons: them and us

Birth rate
Australia: 1.8 children per woman
Papua New Guinea: 4.1
Malaysia: 2.9
Indonesia: 2.4
America: 2.1
Britain: 1.7
Italy: 1.3

Murder rate
Australia: 1.9 per 100 000 people each year
South Africa: 55.9
America: 5.6
New Zealand: 2.5
Britain: 1.6
Italy: 1.5
Japan: 1.0

Median age of population
Australia: 37
Japan: 43
Italy: 42
Britain: 39
America: 36
Indonesia: 26
Papua New Guinea: 20

Life expectancy for females

Australia: A baby girl born now can expect to live till 83 years of age
Hong Kong: 85
Japan: 85
Italy: 83
Britain: 81
America: 80
Malaysia: 76
Indonesia: 69

Enrolled in education

Australia: 83 per cent of people aged between 16 and 19
France: 87 per cent
Britain: 77 per cent
America: 75 per cent
New Zealand: 72 per cent
Malaysia: 55 per cent
Indonesia: 46 per cent

Academic skills

Literacy: Australia's 15 year olds can read better than teens in France, Hong Kong, Japan, Sweden and America, and less well than teens in Canada, Korea and Britain.

Science and maths: Our 15 year olds do better than teens in Italy, America, France and Sweden, and worse than teens in Britain, Japan, Korea and Hong Kong.

Unemployment

Australia's rate of 5 per cent is better than the USA's (6 per cent), Canada's (8), Italy's (9) and France's (10), and equal to Britain's, Sweden's, Japan's and New Zealand's (all 5 per cent).

Cheers

Australia is the number four **wine-exporting** country in the world (Italy is top) and the number 16 **wine-drinking** country, with 22 litres per person per year (France tops this list with 56 litres per person).

Comparisons: men and women

About 51 per cent of our population is **female**; 49 per cent is **male**. The difference happens because men die younger than women — in any year roughly 67 000 men will die compared with 62 000 women.

The **life expectancy** of a boy born this year is 77 and a girl is 83, unless they are Aboriginal, for whom the figures are 60 and 65 respectively.

The average weekly total **earnings** of women is $612; for men it's $898. When hours and types of job are standardised, it appears that women, on average, earn 91 per cent of what men earn: an improvement from 78 per cent in the early 1970s.

Women **hold** 15 per cent of ministerial-level jobs in Australian state and federal government, and 15 per cent of senior management jobs in private enterprise.

The Australian Bureau of Statistics tells us a woman is **more likely** than a man to be: old, living alone, at the movies, using a library, seeing a doctor, seeking a divorce, in a botanic garden, sexually assaulted, walking for exercise, suffering arthritis and asthma, and using contraception.

She is **less likely** than a man to be: murdered, beaten up, robbed, in gaol, watching a sporting event, deaf, playing golf, dying of cancer or injured in an accident.

What's wrong with us

We're not hypochondriacs

Health surveys by the Bureau of Statistics find 82 per cent of Australians saying they are in 'good', 'very good' or 'excellent' health. The most common disorders described are:

1 **Long sightedness:** 27 per cent of the population
2 **Short sightedness:** 22 per cent
3 **Hay fever and allergic rhinitis:** 16 per cent
4 **Back problems:** 15 per cent
5 **Arthritis:** 15 per cent
6 **High blood pressure:** 11 per cent
7 **Asthma:** 11 per cent
8 **Sinusitis:** 11 per cent
9 **Total/partial hearing loss:** 10 per cent
10 **High cholesterol:** 7 per cent
11 **Diabetes:** 4 per cent

The major causes of death are:

1 **Cancer:** 29 per cent of deaths
2 **Heart disease:** 20 per cent
3 **Stroke:** 9 per cent
4 **Lung diseases:** 5 per cent
5 **Accidents:** 4 per cent
6 **Diabetes:** 2 per cent

How we feel

When it comes to **being happy**, we are.

As part of a national health survey in 2002, the Bureau of Statistics slipped in a fundamental question: **How do you feel about your life?** People in 18 000 households were asked to rate their degree of euphoria, using one of the following terms: 'Delighted'; 'Pleased'; 'Mostly satisfied'; 'Mixed'; 'Mostly dissatisfied'; 'Unhappy'; 'Terrible'.

Overall:

12 per cent of Australian adults said they were delighted

31 per cent were pleased

33 per cent were mostly satisfied

Only 1.3 per cent felt terrible.

Apparently, 8 million of us are going around with big smiles on our faces, and most of the rest aren't complaining.

The Bureau then correlated the core question with a bunch of other measures to deconstruct **the components of the 'Good Life'**:

The happiest Australians are people who are hitting their targets. Asked if they had accomplished the tasks they set out to do in the past four weeks, 85 per cent of the sample thought they had. Among people who had achieved what they planned, 47 per cent said they were delighted or pleased with their lives and only 1.5 per cent felt unhappy or terrible. Among people who had **accomplished less** than they desired, only 16 per cent were delighted or pleased, while 13 per cent were feeling unhappy or terrible.

Booze helps! Among people who averaged the equivalent of three glasses of wine a day, 49.7 per cent are delighted or pleased and only 2.2 per cent feel terrible or unhappy. Among people who **never drink**, only 37 per cent are delighted or pleased with their lives and 6 per cent feel unhappy or terrible. The **happiest drinkers** are in a category the ABS calls 'risky' rather than 'moderate', which suggests that many Australians are balancing short-term pleasure against long-term damage.

Smokers are unhappy, but it's not clear what's cause and what's effect. Only 36 per cent of current smokers were delighted or pleased with their lives, while 42 per cent of ex-smokers and 46 per cent of those who have never smoked were in that state of bliss.

A **geographical breakdown** suggests Sydney is the happiest kingdom of them all. In the big smoke, 14.4 per cent of people were delighted with their lives and only 0.9 per cent felt terrible, compared with 11.4 per cent delighted and 2.1 per cent terrible in outback New South Wales, and 11.4 per cent and 1.1 per cent in Melbourne.

In **relationships** the most miserable were separated people (10 per cent felt unhappy or terrible and only 23 per cent were delighted or pleased), while the cheeriest were the marrieds (2.2 per cent unhappy or terrible and 45 per cent delighted or pleased). But the never married were happier than the divorced.

And **baby boomers** aren't as smug as we thought. People aged 40 to 64 are less happy than those 18 to 39 (38 per cent of boomers are delighted or pleased, compared with 49 per cent of Gen-Yers and Xers).

The **obese** are uncomfortable: 37.5 per cent delighted or pleased and 4 per cent feeling terrible or unhappy. People who do lots of exercise every week are blissful: 58.5 per cent delighted or pleased and only 1.7 per cent terrible or unhappy.

Clearly, we still think we're the lucky country.

What Australians believe

In 2005, The Australian National University's Centre for Social Research published 'Australian Social Attitudes: A First Report'. Edited by Shaun Wilson, the report analysed the results of a mail questionnaire completed by 4270 adults. These were the major opinions held by most Australians:

To be **truly Australian**, it is 'fairly important' that you … 'speak English', 92 per cent; 'feel Australian', 91 per cent; 'have Australian citizenship', 89 per cent; 'respect Australia's political institutions and law', 89 per cent; 'be born in Australia', 58 per cent; 'be Christian', 36 per cent.

'The **father** should be as involved in the care of his children as the mother': 90 per cent agree.

'A woman should have the right to choose whether or not she has an **abortion**': 87 per cent agree.

'The gap between those with **high incomes** and those with low incomes is too large': 84 per cent agree.

'Generally speaking, Australia is **a better country** than most other countries': 83 per cent agree.

'When **big businesses** break the law they often go unpunished': 81 per cent agree.

'**Media ownership** in Australia is too concentrated among a few rich families': 81 per cent agree.

'Large **international companies** are doing more and more damage to local businesses in Australia': 75 per cent agree.

'**Immigrants** make Australia open to new ideas and cultures': 74 per cent agree.

'People who receive **welfare benefits** should be under more obligation to work': 73 per cent agree.

'It is better for society if immigrant groups **adapt and blend** into the larger society': 71 per cent agree.

'Television **violence** encourages social violence': 71 per cent agree.

'The **media** should have less power': 70 per cent agree.

'Immigrants are generally good for Australia's **economy**': 69 per cent agree.

'Australia should limit **import of foreign products** to protect the economy': 65 per cent agree.

Which institutions should be **publicly owned**: prisons, 67 per cent; Australia Post, 67 per cent; public transport, 63 per cent; electricity, 60 per cent; Telstra, 57 per cent.

'Television is my main source of **household entertainment**': 67 per cent.

'Commercial television is my daily **source of news and information**': 65 per cent (ABC and SBS 41 per cent; radio 63 per cent; newspapers 40 per cent).

'Management and employees have good relations in my **workplace**': 62 per cent agree.

'Is the **mass media** effective in keeping governments on their toes?': 60 per cent say yes.

'Thinking about the **federal government** in Australia these days, would you say that it is …' run mainly for a few big interests looking out for themselves, 60 per cent; run for the benefit of all the people, 40 per cent.

'Australia should pursue greater economic ties with **Asia**': 56 per cent agree.

'What is most important to your **identity**?' My family, 52 per cent; my occupation, 16 per cent; where in Australia I live, 3 per cent.

'Overall, how satisfied are you with **your job**?': 47 per cent highly satisfied, 11 per cent highly dissatisfied.

'The **death penalty** should be the punishment for murder': 47 per cent agree, 33 per cent disagree.

'Australia's television should give **preference to Australian films** and programs': 46 per cent agree, 24 per cent disagree.

'Government should **redistribute income** from the better-off to those who are less well-off': 44 per cent agree, 30 per cent disagree.

'A **preschool child** is likely to suffer if the mother works': 44 per cent of men agree, 30 per cent disagree; 31 per cent of women agree, 45 per cent disagree.

'The law should recognise **same sex relationships**': 34 per cent agree, 41 per cent disagree.

'The number of **immigrants** allowed into Australia should be': decreased, 38 per cent; the same, 31 per cent; increased, 26 per cent.

'Smoking **marijuana** should not be a criminal offence': 32 per cent agree, 49 per cent disagree.

'Exposure to **foreign films**, music and books causes damage to national and local cultures': 24 per cent agree, 53 per cent disagree.

'If the government had a choice between reducing personal income **taxes** or increasing social spending on services like health and education, which do you think it should be?': Increase social spending, 48 per cent; lower taxes, 28 per cent; stay same as now, 24 per cent.

Over the next ten years, the **national priorities** should be: Maintain a high level of economic growth, 53 per cent; a stable economy, 50 per cent; maintain order in the nation, 37 per cent; give people more say in important government decisions, 37 per cent; progress towards a less impersonal and more human society, 21 per cent; make sure this country has strong defence forces, 20 per cent. (Respondents were allowed two choices.)

What John Howard thinks we believe

1 We live in a very **successful** nation.

2 We do not have much to be **ashamed** of.

3 Australia is **well-regarded** around the world.

4 Individuals should be given a **fair go** if down on their luck but, once helped, should not expect continued community support.

5 Traditional institutions like the family are central but people with alternative views should not be **persecuted**.

6 People should be very tolerant of **diversity**, but also believe in unity when facing a common threat.

7 Society should be **classless**, where a person's worth is determined by personal character and hard work, and not religion, race or social background.

(Source: The prime minister offered that summary of 'core beliefs of average Australians' while launching a Liberal Party magazine called *The Conservative* in September 2005).

Wealth for toil

We're all **getting richer**, but the rich are doing it quicker. A survey by the Bureau of Statistics in 2004 showed that 'in real terms, the **average equalised disposable household income**' of Australians was $510 a week; 2 per cent higher than in 2001 and 15 per cent higher than in 1995.

A more useful statement is that half the population has, after tax, a **disposable income** below $600 a week, while 10 per cent of people earn less than $250 a week and 10 per cent earn more than $950 a week.

Over the ten-year period from 1994 to 2004, says the Bureau, 'there was a 12 per cent increase in the **real mean income** of low-income people, 14 per cent for middle-income people and 16 per cent for high-income people'. Over the same period, **personal debt** has doubled and the average household now spends 9 per cent of its available income on interest repayments.

The group with the **highest income** is couples under 35 without children: they average a combined income of $770 a week after tax, while households containing one parent with dependent children average $355 a week. Clearly we should all become DINKs (dual income, no kids).

Alternatively, we could haunt **antique** stores, bottle shops and auction rooms for a lucky find, such as:

- a **painting** by Frederick McCubbin, Arthur Streeton, or Brett Whiteley: the highest price ever paid at auction for an Australian painting was $2.31 million for McCubbin's 'Bush Idyll' in 1998; followed by $2.03 million for Streeton's 'Sunlight Sweet, Coogee' in 2005; $1.98 million for Whiteley's 'The Jacaranda Tree (in Sydney Harbour)' in 1999; and $1.98 million in 1996 for Eugene Von Guerard's 'View of Geelong' (painted in 1856). Works by John H. Glover, Rupert Bunny, Sidney Nolan, Arthur Boyd, Russell Drysdale and Rover Thomas have also fetched more than a million
- a **1930 penny**, of which only 3000 were made, could be worth $50 000
- an **1854 fourpenny stamp** from Western Australia with a black swan printed upside down, which could be worth $115 000

- a **bottle of Grange** (red wine) more than ten years old, which could be worth more than $5000: in 1999, a bottle of 1951 Grange Hermitage went for $33 600 at an Oddbins auction in Adelaide, while a world record of $124 000 was paid for a complete set of Grange from 1951 to 1994. If you want to buy now and sell in ten years, the best years for Grange lately have been 1986, 1990, 1993 and 1996
- a bottle of **Seppelt 100 Year Old Para Liqueur**, made in 1904 and released in 2004: it cost $1050 a bottle then, making it Australia's most expensive wine at the time of release.

But luck like that won't get you into *BRW* magazine's annual list of Australia's 200 richest people, who are collectively worth $100 billion. They include:

- **James Packer** of Sydney, worth $7.1 billion from casinos, television, publishing, and investments (PBL)
- **Frank Lowy** of Sydney, worth $5.4 billion from shopping centres and investments (Westfield)
- **Richard Pratt** of Melbourne, 'the cardboard box king', worth $5.2 billion from packaging and investments (Visy Industries)
- **Shi Zhengrong** of Sydney and Wuxi, China, worth $3 billion from energy technology (Suntech Power Holdings)
- **Harry Triguboff** of Sydney, worth $2.5 billion from property development (Meriton Apartments).

Australia's richest women are:

- **Gina Rinehart** of Perth, worth $1.8 billion from iron ore royalties
- **Angela Bennett** of Perth, worth $900 million from iron ore royalties
- **Imelda Roche** of Sydney, worth $545 million from investments
- **Naomi Milgrom** of Melbourne, worth $495 million from clothing and property
- **Charlotte Vidor** of Sydney, worth $430 million from property.

Australia's richest families are the:

- **Smorgons** of Melbourne, worth $2.4 billion from manufacturing
- **Libermans** of Melbourne, worth $1.6 billion from investments
- **Besens** of Melbourne, worth $1.4 billion from retail and property.

2

A POTTED HISTORY

Our timeline

BC 40 million

The island we now call Australia breaks free from a much bigger landmass, now known as **Gondwana**.

Before BC 50 000

People arrive from the lands in the north and start **spreading** across the continent.

BC 40 000

Aboriginal people engrave animal images on rocks in the Olary region of South Australia, creating the world's **oldest known** art.

BC 35 000

The **Aborigines** reach Tasmania.

BC 30 000

A long **cold spell** kills off the 'mega fauna': giant wombats (*Diprotodon australis*), emus (*Genyornis newtoni*), goannas (*Megalania prisca*) and lions (*Thylacoleo carnifex*).

BC 12 000

Rising seas separate Tasmania from the mainland.

BC 8000

Rising seas separate **New Guinea** from the mainland.

1422

A Chinese fleet commanded by **Admiral Hong Bau** travels too far to the south and approaches the west coast of a big island that might be Australia.

1523–39

Portuguese sailors under the command of **Cristavao de Mendonca** map the south-west coastline of a big island they call 'Java le grand'.

1606

A Dutch ship, the *Duyfken*, lands on the northern tip of the island (a spot now called **Weipa**) but leaves quickly when a sailor is speared by the locals.

1616

A Dutch captain, **Dirck Hartogh**, lands on the west coast (now Shark Bay), nails a pewter plate to a tree, and names the place 'Eendrachtsland', after his ship.

1642

A Dutch captain, **Abel Tasman**, lands on an island south of the main continent and names it 'Van Diemen's Land', after the Governor of the Dutch East Indies.

1770

An English ship, *HM Bark Endeavour*, commanded by **James Cook**, maps the east coast of a continent the Dutch are calling 'Hollandia Nova'. Cook names the place 'New South Wales'.

1788 (26 January)

An English fleet of eleven ships, commanded by **Arthur Phillip**, delivers 770 convicted criminals plus soldiers, sailors, administrators and families, and establishes a penal colony in what Phillip calls 'Sydney Harbour'.

1789

Convicts perform Australia's first English **play**, *The Recruiting Officer*.

1790

Convict farmer **James Ruse** produces the first successful wheat crop. The Eora, Dharuk and Tharawal people, led by Pemulwuy, begin a resistance to the English colonists, burning crops and killing soldiers. (Pemulwuy is killed in 1802.)

1793

The first eight **free settlers** arrive in Sydney from London.

1794

Thomas Watling, a Scottish convict, completes Australia's first oil painting, 'A Direct North General View of Sydney Cove'.

1795

A German free settler, **Phillip Schaffer**, produces 90 gallons (410 litres) of white 'Rhinewine' at Parramatta.

1798

John Macarthur and **Samuel Marsden** bring merino sheep from South Africa and start a breeding program that ultimately makes wool our major export industry for the next 150 years. The first platypus specimen sent to London is branded a hoax.

1803

The country's first **newspaper**, the *Sydney Gazette*, is published. The first cricket match is played between some free settlers and officers of the supply ship *HMS Calcutta* in Sydney's Hyde Park.

1804

Troops put down a **rebellion** by 300 convicts near Parramatta, with nine rioters shot and six leaders hanged. A new penal colony, later called 'Hobart', is established on the southern island, now called '**Tasmania**'.

1805

The *Sydney Gazette* reports an epidemic of **gambling** by 'chuck farthing', later called 'two-up'.

1808

A military coup, known as the 'rum rebellion', deposes **Governor William Bligh** in Sydney and the NSW Corps runs the town.

1809

Australia's first **post office** opens in the Sydney home of Isaac Nichols, who charges one shilling for each letter he passes on.

1810

Governor **Lachlan Macquarie** arrives to restore London rule. The first official horse race, clockwise round Hyde Park, is held in October.

1813

Explorers **Blaxland**, **Lawson** and **Wentworth** cross the Blue Mountains west of Sydney and open a path to the country's interior.

1814

Governor Macquarie begins an 'extravagant' building program and accepts a recommendation from the explorer **Matthew Flinders** that the continent be named 'Australia'.

1817

Australia's first bank, the **Bank of New South Wales** (now called Westpac) opens for business.

1819

The first **book** by an Australian, *A Statistical, Historical and Political Description of the Colony of New South Wales* by William Charles Wentworth, is published.

1825

A new penal colony, to be called '**Brisbane**', is established in the north to handle the most difficult convicts.

1829

The English establish the Swan River military base on the west coast, to be called '**Perth**'. Rugby football is first played — by soldiers at the Sydney barracks.

1831

The Sydney *Herald* is published (later called the *Sydney Morning Herald*).

1835

John Batman uses flour and blankets to 'buy' land from Aboriginal people at Port Phillip and establishes a settlement to be called '**Melbourne**'.

1836

Free settlers from Britain establish a community on the mid-southern coast of Australia, to be called '**Adelaide**'.

1838

Seven white settlers are executed for the massacre of 28 Aborigines at **Myall Creek** in northern New South Wales.

1843

The first elected **Legislative Council** shares power with the Governor of New South Wales.

1851

Victoria becomes a separate colony from New South Wales. **Edward Hargraves** announces he has found gold west of the Blue Mountains, starting a gold rush. The University of Sydney is founded with three lecturers and twenty-four students. A second gold rush begins in Victoria after a discovery near Ballarat, north-west of Melbourne. (Ultimately, the Victorian goldfields produce eight times as much gold as the New South Wales fields.) The first Chinese settlers arrive in search of gold and stay to run market gardens and restaurants.

1854

On 3 December, Victorian gold prospectors gather in the **Eureka Stockade** under their own Southern Cross flag, protesting police corruption and the cost of mining licences. Government troops put down the rebellion; nearly forty diggers and five troopers are killed and another hundred diggers are imprisoned.

1856

Melbourne stonemasons are given an **eight-hour** working day, pioneering improved conditions for other labourers. New South Wales beats Victoria in the first inter-colony **cricket** match, played in Melbourne.

1858

The population of the colonies reaches **one million**.

1859

The first **rabbits** are imported into Victoria by Thomas Austin, to make him 'feel at home'. They become a national plague.

1861

The first Melbourne Cup horse race is won by **Archer**.

1865

The first **stock exchange** opens in Melbourne (opens in Sydney in 1871). Scottish baker William Arnott opens a biscuit factory in Newcastle and goes on to make Tim Tam, Sao, Iced VoVo, Jatz and Milk Arrowroot biscuits.

1866

The New South Wales Colonial Secretary, **Henry Parkes**, greatly reduces state aid to religious schools.

1868

The final shipment of **convicts**, making a national total of 159 000, reaches Australia, landing in Fremantle (transportation to the east coast ended in 1852). Maria Smith develops the Granny Smith long-lasting green apple in her garden at Eastwood, Sydney.

1870

The first **Australian Rules** football match is played in Melbourne between Scotch College and Melbourne Church of England Grammar School, with forty players per side.

1872

Victoria introduces **compulsory primary school** education for all children (the other colonies follow by 1895). Fur cutter Benjamin Dunkerly starts using rabbit skins to make **Akubra** hats in Tasmania.

1877

Australia wins the first **Test** against England at the Melbourne Cricket Ground.

1879

The world's first officially declared **National Park** opens near Sutherland, south of Sydney. The first recordings of the human voice, on the **Edison phonograph**, are heard in Sydney, two years after Thomas Edison introduced the device in America.

1880

Ned Kelly's bushranger gang is captured in Victoria and Kelly is later hanged. The first **telephone** exchange opens in Melbourne, with forty-four subscribers.

1883

A **train service** begins between Sydney and Melbourne.

1890

The Carlton and United Brewery in Melbourne starts making **Victoria Bitter**, destined to become our most popular beer.

1892

The **Australian Labour Party** (spelling changed to 'Labor' in 1907) is formed in four cities by unionists disgruntled by the defeat of strikes in the shearing and shipping industries.

1894

Women get the right to **vote** in South Australian elections.

1895

Banjo Paterson writes the words to '**Waltzing Matilda**' while staying at a property near Winton, Queensland.

1896

The **first moving pictures** are projected onto a screen by American magician Carl Hertz at the Tivoli Theatre, Melbourne. Marius Sestier, an agent of the Lumiere Brothers in Paris, makes the first films in Sydney and Melbourne. Melbourne engineer Herbert Thomson builds Australia's first **car**: steam-powered (he goes out of business in 1912).

1897

A convention of politicians from the six colonies draw up a draft **constitution** for a united Australia. The first petrol-powered motor car, called '**The Hertel**', is imported.

1899

Australia sends 16 000 troops to South Africa to help Britain in the **Boer War**: by 1902, 251 are killed and 267 are dead from disease.

1900

Referendums in every colony support **federation**.

1901

Australia becomes a Federation with six states. **Edmund Barton** becomes the prime minister in the first national election. The first **federal parliament** opens in Melbourne and passes an immigration restriction bill, which becomes known as the 'White Australia Policy'. A parliamentary committee chooses, from 32 823 entries, a **flag** for Australia: six stars on dark blue background with Britain's Union Jack in the top-left corner.

1904

An 1800-kilometre '**rabbit-proof fence**' is completed in Western Australia.

1906

The world's first surf lifesaving club is formed at **Bondi Beach** in Sydney. The first full-length movie, **The Story of the Kelly Gang**, is made in Victoria.

1908

South Sydney wins the first **rugby league** premiership.

1911

The town of Palmerston on the north coast of the continent is renamed '**Darwin**' and it becomes the capital of the Northern Territory, which is controlled by the federal government.

1912

John Duigan flies the first successful Australian-designed and built **aircraft** near Kyneton in Victoria. The federal government sets up the **Commonwealth Bank of Australia**, intended to put community service ahead of greed, and it is based in Sydney.

1913

The national capital, **Canberra**, is officially named.

1914

On 4 August, Australia joins Britain in declaring **war** on Germany.

1915

On 25 April, the Australia and New Zealand Army Corps (**ANZAC**) launches an attack at Gallipoli in southern Turkey, but withdraws eight months later after 8500 are killed. The Queensland government makes **voting** in state elections compulsory (joined by the federal government in 1924). A Hawaiian, Duke Kahanamoku, introduces **surfboard** riding at Harbord Beach in Sydney.

1916

A referendum rejects **conscription** as a means of boosting the war effort.

1918

On 11 November, the **Great War** officially ends: 60 500 Australians were killed during its campaigns. The nation's population reaches five million.

1919

Ross and Keith Smith take 25 days to make the first flight from Britain to Australia.

1922

Queensland and Northern Territory Aerial Services (**QANTAS**) offers the first commercial flights.

1923

Vegemite, a black spread made from the waste products of beer manufacture, goes on sale in Victoria. The first **radio station**, 2SB (later renamed 2BL), starts broadcasting in Sydney.

1924

The American **Kellogg's** company starts making Corn Flakes in Sydney.

1927

The **Australian Council of Trade Unions**, based in Melbourne, is formed. The federal parliament moves to Canberra.

1928

The nation's first **traffic lights** are switched on in Melbourne. The Sanitarium Health Food Agency launches **Weet-Bix**.

1929

The **Speedo** swimming costume is first made by MacRae Knitting Mills in Sydney.

1932

The **Sydney Harbour Bridge** opens. Australia's favourite racehorse, **Phar Lap**, dies suddenly in America (poisoning suspected).

1933

Publisher Frank Packer launches the *Australian Women's Weekly*. The world's first **milk bar**, offering milkshakes for 4 pence, opens in Martin Place in Sydney.

1935

A meringue and cream dessert served at Perth's Esplanade Hotel is named the '**Pavlova**'. The **cane toad** is introduced in Queensland to eat cane beetles (but it eats everything else).

1936

The last known **Thylacine** (Tasmanian tiger) dies in Hobart Zoo (alleged sightings are still sporadically reported).

1938

First **Coca-Cola** bottling plant opens in Waterloo in Sydney.

1939

On 3 September, Australia joins Britain in declaring **war** on Germany.

1941

Johnson + Johnson builds Australia's first **Band-Aid** factory in Sydney.

1942

On 19 February, Japanese planes **bomb Darwin**, killing 243.

1943

The first **women** (Enid Lyons and Dorothy Tangney) are elected to the federal parliament. The Commonwealth Serum Laboratories in Melbourne starts the world's first mass production of **antibiotics** (penicillin).

1944

Robert Menzies forms the **Liberal Party**.

1945

On 15 August, **Japan surrenders**, ending the war after the death of 39 500 Australians.

1946

The federal government introduces a massive **immigration** program from Europe, under the slogan 'populate or perish'. It adds three million to the population by 1980.

1948

The first **Holden** car goes on sale for £760. Lance Hill opens a factory to make **Hills Hoist** clothes lines.

1949

The federal Labor government sets up a spy agency, the Australian Security Intelligence Organisation (**ASIO**). The Snowy Mountains **Hydro-Electric Scheme** begins (one of the world's biggest engineering projects, employing 100 000 people and when completed in 1974 providing power and water to NSW and Victoria). The Liberal Party, in coalition with the Country Party (later renamed the National Party), is elected as the federal government, staying in power for 23 years.

1950

Australia sends troops to join America in fighting **North Korea** (339 Australians are killed by 1953).

1951

The NSW government introduces the world's first paid **sick leave** and paid long service leave. Frank McEnroe invents the **Chiko Roll** in Bendigo in Victoria. Near Adelaide, Max Schubert creates Penfold's **Grange Hermitage**, destined to become Australia's greatest red wine.

1952

Mervyn Victor Richardson invents the **Victa** rotary lawnmower in Concord, Sydney. The Sydney company Malley introduces the **Esky** drink cooler.

1953

The first Gaggia **espresso machine** imported from Italy arrives at the University Coffee Shop in Carlton, Melbourne, launching a coffee craze across Australia's suburbs. Ted Street develops the **Paddle Pop** at Corrimal, near Sydney. Samuel Taylor Pty Ltd introduces **Mortein** fly spray in a pressure pack (first advertised on television by 'Louie The Fly' in 1957).

1955

Pub **drinking hours** in New South Wales are extended from 6 pm closing to 10 pm closing (Victoria follows in 1966). Barry Humphries first performs in Melbourne as **Edna Everage**. Ray Lawler's play, *Summer of the Seventeenth Doll*, about Queensland cane cutters, opens in Melbourne.

1956

On 16 September, Channel TCN 9 in Sydney makes the first television broadcast with **Bruce Gyngell** saying, 'Ladies and gentlemen, good evening and welcome to television'. In November, Melbourne hosts the **Olympics**. New South Wales legalises **poker machines** in clubs. '**Rock around the Clock**' by Bill Haley, the first rock and roll single released on 45 rpm, sells 150 000 copies.

1957

The first Australian-made rock and roll record, *You Hit the Wrong Note, Billy Goat* by **Johnny O'Keefe**, goes on sale; being the last 78 rpm single, it's a flop. Danish architect **Jøern Utzon** wins the competition to design the Sydney Opera House.

1958

Panadol (paracetamol) goes on sale, ultimately becoming Australia's largest-selling painkiller. **Qantas** launches the first around-the-world jet service, taking five days to go from Sydney to London via the United States. The first **Top 40** sales chart of recorded music singles is published by Sydney's 2UE. Slim Dusty's '**Pub With No Beer**' becomes the first locally written and recorded single to reach number one.

1959

The population reaches **ten million**. South Coast, just south-east of Brisbane, renames itself the '**City of Gold Coast**' and encourages high-rise developments near its main beach, Surfers Paradise. Aboriginal artist **Albert Namatjira** dies in gaol, while serving a six-month sentence for supplying alcohol to a relative.

1960

Australia's first **ten pin** bowling alley opens in Hurstville in Sydney. **Fluoride** is added into Sydney's water supply (other states follow within five years). Rolf Harris's '**Tie Me Kangaroo Down, Sport**' is a hit in Britain.

1961

The contraceptive **pill** is approved for prescribing by doctors. The government-owned Totalisator Agency Board (**TAB**) provides the first legal off-course betting on horse races, initially in Melbourne.

1962

Australia's **Rod Laver** makes the tennis 'grand slam', becoming men's singles champion at Wimbledon, the US Open, the French Open and the Australian Open. The Commonwealth Serum Laboratories develops snake bite **antivenene**. Australia's first skyscraper, the 25-storey **AMP Building** on Sydney Harbour, is completed. Australian 'advisers' sent to join US troops to train **South Vietnamese combatants** in their war against North Vietnam.

1963

The 250 000th immigrant from **Italy**, Antonia Bellomarino, steps off the *Neptunia* in Melbourne and receives a set of silver cutlery.

1964

The **Beatles** tour Australia. Bernard 'Midget' Farrelly wins the world's first **surfing championships** at Manly Beach in Sydney. Rupert Murdoch launches a national daily newspaper, *The Australian*. The editors of the satire magazine *Oz*, Richard Neville, Richard Walsh and Martin Sharp, are sentenced to a six-month gaol term for obscenity (later overturned on appeal).

1965

The federal government introduces **conscription** for randomly selected 20-year-old males, to serve two years' national service in the army. The government sends more troops to **Vietnam** (496 are killed by 1972 when Australia withdraws). The Australian crime series '**Homicide**' starts on Channel 7 (and continues until 1975). In Adelaide, **Roma Mitchell** becomes Australia's first female judge.

1966

On 14 February, the **currency changes** from pounds, shillings and pence to dollars and cents (there were 12 pence in a shilling and 20 shillings in a pound). '**Play School**' starts on ABC television. Robert **Menzies retires** as prime minister after a record 16 years.

1967

In a **referendum**, 90 per cent of Australians vote to give full citizenship rights to Aboriginal people. Thomas Angove of South Australia develops the **wine cask** (a bladder in a box). In Melbourne, Ronald Ryan becomes the last person to be **hanged** in Australia. In December, Prime Minister **Harold Holt** disappears while swimming off Portsea in Victoria.

1968

Australia's first **heart transplant** operation at Sydney's St Vincent's Hospital is declared a success; the patient survives 45 days. The first **Kentucky Fried Chicken** store opens in Guildford in Sydney. **Mail deliveries** go from twice a day to once a day. In Sydney, police start using '**the breathalyser**' to test for drink-driving.

1969

South Australia legalises medically supervised **abortions** (followed by New South Wales and Victoria in 1972 and Queensland in 1986). **Rallies** against Australia's involvement in the Vietnam War are held in every state capital. In Sydney, the rock musical *Hair* features the first mass nude scene on stage.

1970

Germaine Greer publishes *The Female Eunuch*, arguing that women's liberation means a happier life for women and men. Adelaide holds its first **Arts Festival**.

1971

Queenslander **Neville Bonner** is appointed to fill a Liberal Party vacancy in the Senate, becoming the first Aboriginal member of parliament. The first **McDonald's** store opens in Yagoona in Sydney. **Anti-apartheid** protesters disrupt cricket and football matches when white South African teams are playing. The NSW Builders Labourers Federation imposes '**green bans**' to prevent development in Sydney's historic Rocks area.

1972

The first issue of **Cleo**, a magazine for young women, is launched, with a nude male centrefold. Tasmanians form the world's first '**Green**' political party. The Labor Party, led by **Gough Whitlam**, is elected as the federal government on 2 December; within a year it ends conscription, removes the last vestiges of the White Australia Policy, makes university education free and lowers the voting age from 21 to 18.

1973

The **Sydney Opera House** opens after 16 years of construction. **Patrick White** becomes the first Australian to win the Nobel Prize for literature. The TV soap '**Number 96**' presents the first bare breasts and the first gay kiss on prime-time television. Australia's first legal casino opens at **Wrest Point** in Tasmania.

1974

American Express and BankCard introduce the first widely available **credit cards**. Inflation reaches 16 per cent. Chardonnay grapes are planted in commercial quantities by **Leeuwin Estate** vineyard in Margaret River, south of Perth. The federal government bans **cigarette advertising** on television. 'Advance Australia Fair' joins 'God Save the Queen' as an alternative **national anthem**. The first **FM radio** stations begin broadcasting in Sydney and Melbourne. **Cyclone Tracy** devastates Darwin.

1975

Colour TV sets go on sale. Melbourne philosopher Peter Singer publishes his book *Animal Liberation*, starting a worldwide movement. The measurement system changes from imperial (inches, ounces, gallons) to **metric** (centimetres, grams, litres): there were 12 inches in a foot, 3 feet in a yard and 1760 yards in a mile; 16 ounces in a pound; eight pints in a gallon; and boiling point was 212 degrees Fahrenheit. *Picnic At Hanging Rock* leads a boom in Australian film-making.

1975

On 11 November, Governor-General John Kerr **dismisses** the Whitlam Government after the Liberal Opposition refuses to pass finance bills in the Senate. The Liberals, under Malcolm Fraser, win the ensuing election. The ABC launches radio **2JJ**, the first non-commercial rock music station, in Sydney (it becomes Triple J and goes national in 1995).

1976

The *Family Law Act*, introduced by Labor to allow **no-fault** divorce, comes into force: there are 63 000 divorces in the first year (there were only 16 000 in 1975). The first '**boat people**' start arriving from Vietnam, welcomed by the federal government. South Australia **decriminalises homosexuality** (New South Wales follows in 1984).

1977

Former Liberal Party Senator Don Chipp forms the **Australian Democrat Party** as a middle path between Liberal and Labor, to 'keep the bastards honest'. In a referendum, Australians choose 'Advance Australia Fair' as their **national anthem**. Queensland abolishes **death duties** (followed within three years by the other states and Canberra). Kerry Packer introduces **World Series Cricket**, aka 'the cricket circus'.

1978

A team, led by Graeme Clark of Melbourne University, invents '**the bionic ear**', an implant that can defeat deafness. An American, Ross McDonald, introduces the Weber **portable barbecue**, allowing urban Australians to have barbies on the balcony.

1979

The first video cassette recorders (**VCR**) go on sale. **Coffee consumption surpasses tea consumption**. The federal government declares the **Great Barrier Reef** a national park to stop the Queensland Government from allowing oil exploration there. **Pam O'Neill** becomes the first woman jockey to ride against men (at Moonee Valley in Melbourne).

1980

A baby, **Azaria Chamberlain**, goes missing at Ayers Rock camping ground. Her mother, Lindy, says a dingo took her (in 1982, Lindy Chamberlain is convicted of murder, but gets a full pardon in 1987). The first 'multicultural' TV network, **SBS**, begins broadcasting.

1981

The population reaches 15 million. The first automatic teller machines (**ATMs**) are installed outside banks. In Melbourne, Carl Wood and Christopher Chen develop a technology that produces the world's first **test-tube twins** (and in 1984, the first frozen embryo baby).

1983

Unemployment reaches 10 per cent. Labor under **Bob Hawke** wins the federal election, then intervenes to prevent the Tasmanian Government flooding the Franklin wilderness after a campaign by conservationists. The Australian **dollar is floated** on world markets as part of economic deregulation. A yacht owned by businessman Alan Bond takes the **America's Cup** from the Americans for the first time in 132 years. Cliff Young, aged 61, wins the Sydney to Melbourne **walking marathon** with a time of 5 days and 15 hours. Men At Work's **'Down Under'** reaches number one in Britain and America. The first Australian death from **AIDS** is recorded at Melbourne's Prince Henry Hospital.

1984

The first compact discs (**CDs**) go on sale, ultimately replacing vinyl recordings. The federal government introduces a law banning **discrimination** on the grounds of sex.

1985

The soap '**Neighbours'** starts on Channel 7 (relaunched in 1986 on Channel 10). Australia's biggest media owner, Rupert Murdoch, becomes a **US citizen**. Ayers Rock is handed back to its original owners and renamed **Uluru**.

1986

The first **mobile phone** goes on sale. *Crocodile Dundee* becomes the most successful film ever made in Australia.

1987

In October, a stock market **crash** ends the 1980s business boom.

1988

On 26 January, a crowd of 1.5 million gathers round Sydney Harbour to celebrate **200 years** of white settlement. Sydney's **Kay Cottee** becomes the first woman to sail solo non-stop around the world.

1989

Queen Elizabeth II **stops** awarding imperial honours (knighthoods) to Australians.

1990

The first '**Internet**' linkup is established between computers at the CSIRO and universities; it's called 'AARNet' (Australian Academic and Research Network).

1991

Treasurer **Paul Keating** replaces Bob Hawke as prime minister. Arnott's is taken over by the US company Campbells. **'Bananas in Pyjamas'** get their own show on ABC television.

1992

The High Court rules that **Eddie Mabo** and islanders from Torres Strait have 'native title' to their land.

1994

The 'native title' bill becomes law, granting Aborigines ownership of traditional lands; the High Court rules in '**the Wik case**' that native title rights to land can co-exist with the rights of pastoralists. The phone company, **Telstra**, starts changing all Australia's phone numbers from six or seven digits to eight digits.

1995

Pay TV (delivered by cable or satellite) begins. The Australian **film industry** enjoys a brief revival with the success of *Muriel's Wedding*, *The Adventures of Priscilla, Queen of the Desert* and *Babe*.

1996

The Liberals, under **John Howard**, win federal government from Labor. Tasmanian **Bob Brown** is elected as the first Green senator in federal parliament. After the massacre of 36 people in a random attack at **Port Arthur** in Tasmania, Prime Minister Howard introduces national anti-gun laws. The Northern Territory government legalises **euthanasia**, or 'the right to die' under medical supervision, but is overruled by federal parliament. During the year, 7492 people, most seeking **asylum**, are placed in detention centres or on the island of Nauru.

1997

Conservative Queensland politician Pauline Hanson launches the **One Nation Party**, committed to cutting immigration and reducing assistance to Aboriginal people. **Ted Matthews**, the last surviving ANZAC who landed at Gallipoli in 1915, dies in Sydney at the age of 101. **Michael Hutchence**, lead singer with the band INXS, dies in Sydney aged 37, apparently after hanging himself.

1999

Australians vote 'No' (55 per cent of the vote) in a referendum on a **republic**; 67 per cent of Canberrans vote 'Yes'. Australian troops help **East Timor** gain independence from Indonesia.

2000

Sydney hosts the **Olympics**. The federal government introduces a Goods and Services Tax (**GST**) of 10 per cent, with fresh foods exempt.

2001

A Norwegian ship called *Tampa* rescues 438 would-be illegal immigrants when their boat from Indonesia sinks off the Western Australian coast; the Australian Navy takes the boat people to the island of **Nauru** and the federal government introduces a policy of 'mandatory detention of unauthorised arrivals' to deter people-smuggling. **Ansett Airlines**, founded in 1936, goes bankrupt.

2002

Eighty-eight Australians are among 202 people killed by car bombs placed by religious fundamentalists at **Kuta Beach** in Bali, Indonesia. Macintosh launches a portable music player called the **iPod**, which becomes the most popular MP3 device in Australia (one million sold within two years).

2003

The **population** reaches 20 million. Australia sends troops to join America in removing **Saddam Hussein** from power in Iraq.

2004

Australia wins 17 gold medals, its highest total ever, at the **Athens Olympics**. John Howard wins government again, defeating Labor's Mark Latham, who retires from politics. Kim Beazley becomes Labor leader. After only six years on the market, Digital Video Discs (**DVDs**), which can store hours of bonus features, replace videotapes as the preferred way to watch movies at home.

2005

The federal government softens its policy on **asylum seekers** detained within Australia and releases several long-term detainees, but changes border laws to require all arriving asylum seekers to be processed offshore. It also changes **industrial relations** laws to make it easier for companies to dismiss employees.

2006

The economy **booms** because of high world prices for iron ore, coal and gold, but China and India begin to develop alternatives to buying from Australia.

2007

John Howard **retires** as prime minister, replaced by Peter Costello.

2009

Australia becomes **a republic**, with John Howard its first president.

3

PECULIARLY
OURS

Symbols

Anthem: 'Advance Australia Fair' (*see* page 109) by Peter Dodds McCormick was written in 1878 and approved by referendum to replace 'God Save the Queen' in 1977

Coat of arms: a shield divided into six states, supported by a red kangaroo and an emu, was declared in 1912

Colours: green and gold, declared in 1984

Flags: the Blue Ensign displays one large white star and a five-star Southern Cross on a navy blue background with a British Union Jack in the top-left corner. It was chosen in 1901 from 32 823 entries in a design contest, and officially declared in 1953. The Aboriginal flag, a yellow sun on a horizontally divided background of black (the night sky) and red (the earth), was designed by Harold Thomas and officially included in the *Flags Act* in 1995

Flower: the golden wattle, *Acacia pycnantha*, declared 1913

Gemstone: the opal, declared 1993

Honours: the highest awarded by the Australian Government is the AC, the Companion of the Order of Australia (up to 25 are given each year). Next comes AO, Officer of the Order of Australia; AM, Member of the Order of Australia; and OAM, Medal of the Order of Australia

Dish: spaghetti bolognese (cooked most often at home and ordered most often when eating out)

Drink: at home, instant coffee; outside the house, cappuccino

Tipple: with food, chardonnay (Queen Adelaide top brand); without food, beer (Victoria Bitter top brand)

Condiments: tomato sauce (in 90 per cent of households); soy sauce (in 70 per cent of households)

Spreads: Vegemite; Nutella

Fast foods: pizza; hamburgers

Footwear: thongs

Nuisance: blowfly

Salute: waving the fly away

Greeting: G'day

Australian values

Bet on anything. Australians are gambling addicts, starting from the epidemic of 'chuck farthing' (two-up) reported by the *Sydney Gazette* in 1805. Every year we lose $15 billion on games of chance, which means that on average every adult throws away $1000 a year, mainly on poker machines, casinos, horse racing, and lotteries (such as Lotto, scratch and the pools). State governments gain 12 per cent of their revenue from taxes on gambling.

The cultural cringe. A belief, prevalent until the 1970s, that any work done by Australians would inevitably be inferior to the work of British and American people, and that we needed them to teach us how to be 'world class'.

The cultural strut. A belief, growing since the 1970s, that we have nothing to learn from other countries because Australians are the best in the world at sport, acting, directing, winemaking, modelling and music. (Since 2003 there has been a small revival in the cultural cringe, as Australians avoid their own dramas on television and their own movies at the cinema.)

Early adopting. Australians embrace new communications technology faster than the citizens of any other country. Colour television, the CD player, the VCR, the mobile phone, and the DVD player had all spread to more than half the nation's homes within eight years of their introduction. The only gadget that failed to seize our imagination was subscription TV (delivered by cable or satellite), which seems stuck at 25 per cent penetration — probably because we have too many other sources of amusement.

Fair go. It's what everyone is entitled to, but particularly the little Aussie battler. We don't believe there is a class structure. There should be no such thing as inherited privilege in this country — unless it's my kids.

Laconic understatement. 'Not too bad' means 'excellent'. 'That'll do' means 'job well done'. 'You're not wrong' means 'I wholeheartedly agree'. 'Bit off colour' or 'not 100 per cent' means 'gravely ill'.

Loving to lose. There's a theory that Australia, founded by rejects from British society, is more inclined to celebrate failure than success, with a national holiday devoted to a military fiasco (Anzac Day), a hero hanged after bungling a bank robbery (Ned Kelly), an alternative anthem about a sheep thief who commits suicide ('Waltzing Matilda'), and a film industry that keeps making self-critical movies that nobody goes to see.

The Lucky Country. The title of a 1964 book by Donald Horne, who argued that Australians were taking the country's natural advantages for granted and should improve their national management. His ironic meaning is now lost, and the term is a boast about our blessings.

Mateship. Loyalty to friends, workmates and people of the same class, manifested particularly in the principle that you never dob. Reporting someone to the authorities, even when you know they are committing serious crimes, has been a no-no since convict days because, after all, whose side are you on?

Outback nostalgia. Since 85 per cent of Australians live within fifty kilometres of the sea, our self-image as a nation of bush battlers is a century out of date. Suburbanites identify with the outback by wearing Akubra hats and using overpowered four-wheel drives to take the kids to school, where bush ballads are still taught as Australian poetry. The mythology permeates everyday speech: 'bush telegraph' (rumours), 'bush lawyer' (untrained expert), 'bushwalking' (getting exercise in a forested area), 'bush medicine' (treatments known to Aboriginal people), 'go bush' (disappear), 'bush tucker' (edible native plants such as quandongs and lemon myrtle and edible animals such as kangaroo and crocodile), and 'What do you think this is — bush week?' (a mythical period when the usual social restraints do not apply).

Reconciliation. Some Australians believe the government should apologise to Aboriginal people for taking their land in the 18th and 19th centuries, and for taking their children in the 20th century (a policy of assimilation condemned in *The Stolen Generations Report* issued in 1996 by the Human Rights and Equal Opportunity Commission). Other Australians believe governments have already done enough to relieve poverty and ill-health in Aboriginal communities and they should now be able to look after themselves. The current prime minister, John Howard, leans towards the latter view.

Self-deprecating humour. Q: What's an Aussie man's idea of foreplay? A: Are you awake, love? Q: Why do Aussie men come so quickly? A: So they can get to the pub and tell their mates about it.

She'll be right. The phrase implies a laid-back approach to work and relationships, signifying calm optimism or complacent fatalism. The sentiment underlies other slogans such as 'No worries'; 'Don't get your knickers in a knot'; 'Settle down'; 'Get real'; 'Give it a rest'; and 'I'd rather be sailing'. The prime minister, John Howard, expressed the notion during the 1999 election campaign when he said Australians wanted to be 'relaxed and comfortable'. After the events of 11 September 2001, this changed to 'alert but not alarmed'.

Tall poppy syndrome. A tendency to ridicule those who display arrogance about their wealth, fame or success. It often involves the recounting of scandals about politicians, entertainers and businesspeople — some of which may be true.

Wordplay. The creation of diminutives by adding '-ie' or '-o' or '-a', as in 'We thought we'd give the kiddies their Chrissie pressies by the barbie this year, so come round for brekkie and bring your cossie, a few tinnies and something to stop the mossies'. Or 'The journo reckons the garbo's off on compo because he went troppo'. Or 'Did you see that Kezza [Kerry Packer] met Chazza [Prince Charles] and they talked about Bazza [Barry McKenzie]?'

We also enjoy **reverse nicknames** — a red-haired person called Bluey, a dark-haired person called Snowy, a short person called Lofty. And rhyming slang: 'Have a captain at that' (Captain Cook = look); 'Let's go to the rubbidy' (rubbidy dub = pub); 'Me old china' (china plate = mate).

The yellow peril. Some Australians believe we should seek 'engagement with Asia', since we are geographically closer to China, Indonesia and Malaysia than we are to Britain or the United States, and we have embraced Thai, Chinese and Japanese influences in our cooking culture. Other Australians fear 'Asianisation' will mean immigrants who work harder than Australians and immigrants' children who beat local children at school and university. People of Asian background are less than 5 per cent of the population.

How we speak

Australia has **226 languages**. After English, the most popular are Italian (spoken at home by 354 000 people), Greek (264 000), Cantonese (225 000) and Arabic (209 000).

Our version of English contains hundreds of expressions unfamiliar to Americans, Brits, Canadians, South Africans and New Zealanders. Derived from Aboriginal languages*, or from now-vanished English, Scottish or Irish dialects, or from jokes only we understand, they include:

Ang on, or **Ang about**: wait a moment.

Avago ya mug: give it a try, don't hold back.

Banana republic: what former treasurer Paul Keating thought Australia was in danger of becoming if we didn't fix our economy.

Barra: short for barramundi*, a fish native to northern waters.

Barrack: to cheer a team or player (the US equivalent is 'root', which has a different meaning here, so that 'root, root, root for the home team' sounds to us like an invitation to an orgy).

Battler: hard-working poor person.

Bindi-eye*: a painful thorn encountered by bare feet in summer grass.

Blind Freddy: the person who can immediately see the bleedin' obvious: 'Blind Freddy can tell he's a bludger.'

Bloke: a down-to-earth man; drinking beer and watching footy displays 'blokiness'.

Bludger: a lazy person who takes advantage of others.

Blue: an argument or fight, as in 'get in a blue' (but 'true blue' means 'honest' or 'fair dinkum').

Bodgie: in the 1950s, a flashy teenage boy with groomed hair (the self-confident politician Bob Hawke was called 'the silver bodgie'); the female equivalent is 'widgie'. Referring to an object, bodgie can mean 'fake' or 'poorly constructed'.

Bogan: an unfashionable working-class person. The term was popularised by the Melbourne schoolgirl character Kylie Mole in the TV series 'The Comedy Company'.

Boofy: dumb and masculine, as in 'big boofy bloke', derived from a comic strip character called Boofhead. It's the opposite of poofy.

Buckley's chance: highly unlikely: 'You've got Buckley's of ever getting him to shout.'

Budgie: short for budgerigar*, a small colourful native bird (a tight swimming costume on a man is known as a 'budgie smuggler'; Kylie Minogue is 'the singing budgie').

Cactus: defeated, in big trouble: 'If she finds out, you're cactus.'

Chuck a wobbly: go into a rage.

Chunder: vomit, spew, technicolour yawn, go the big spit, drive the porcelain bus.

Clayton's: a safe alternative, derived from Clayton's tonic, 'the drink you have when you're not having a drink'.

Coo-ee*: a cry to attract attention in the bush.

Corroboree*: a ritual gathering; the late 20th-century family habit of watching a movie on television at 8.30 pm every Sunday night was known as 'the national corroboree'.

Cot-case: ill, often mentally.

Crikey: 'Good heavens!'

Crook: sick or angry: 'Don't go crook on me', or 'I'm feeling crook today.'

Dag: an unfashionable person, derived from a term for the matted wool around a sheep's anus.

Daks: trousers.

Dead set: completely or honestly: 'Dead set, Mum, I'm dead set gonna finish it.'

Didgeridoo*: long hollow wooden tube that amplifies chanting.

Dog's breakfast: a mess, same as 'mad woman's breakfast', or 'mad woman's knitting'.

Donkey vote: a way of demonstrating ignorance or apathy that is only possible because of Australia's compulsory preferential system. A donkey voter unthinkingly numbers the candidates from the top of the card to the bottom.

Dorothy Dixer: a question you have asked someone to put to you because you already know the answer. The term, derived from a newspaper columnist who solved the romantic problems of her readers, is used most often in parliament, where political leaders eagerly respond to Dorothy Dixers from their own supporters.

Dreaming: Aboriginal legends, sometimes called 'alcheringa'.

Drongo: a boring fool, derived from the name of an unsuccessful Melbourne race horse in the 1920s; similar to 'nong', 'drip', 'dickhead', 'dropkick', 'galah' and 'silly nana'.

Drover's dog: the animal helped to move cattle across the outback, but now the term means 'any random individual'. Forced to hand over the Labor leadership to Bob Hawke in 1983, Bill Hayden said, 'I believe that a drover's dog could lead the Labor Party to victory, the way the country is and the way the opinion polls are showing up for the Labor Party.'

Duco: the shiny paintwork on a car.

Dunny: outdoor toilet, but '. . . bangs like a dunny door' is a synonym for promiscuity.

Fair enough: agreed, acceptable; often preceded by 'Goodo'.

Few bricks short of a load: stupid or mad; similar to 'not playing with a full deck', 'lights on but nobody's home', 'a few sandwiches short of a picnic' and 'some roos loose in the top paddock'.

Flake out: to have a rest, collapse, fall asleep.

Furphy: an implausible story, often about a famous person.

Gutful: enough.

Hoon: a noisy lair.

Jackaroo: a man who goes to work with horses, cattle or sheep on a country property; the female equivalent is a 'jillaroo'.

Koori: an Aboriginal person from southern New South Wales or Victoria; the Queensland equivalent is 'Murri', and the South Australian is 'Nunga'.

Kn'oath: definitely (short for 'fucken oath').

Lair: a show-off; 'mug lair': a stupid show-off.

Larrikin: a person with a mischievous sense of humour.

Mate: friend; sometimes used to reassure a colleague before you betray him.

Mob: tribe or group of emotionally connected companions: 'Is he one of your mob?'

Mongrel: dishonest person, bastard.

Ocker: exaggeratedly Australian.

Onya: congratulations, short for 'good on you'.

Pea: the chosen one, the most likely winner: 'She's the pea.'

Pom: English person, derived from 'pomegranate', for the red cheeks of the new arrivals.

Poofter: homosexual (also 'willy woofter', 'queer', 'pillowbiter').

Ratbag: an eccentric person.

Rat's: don't care: 'I couldn't give a rat's (arse) about that.'

Recession we had to have: former treasurer Paul Keating's stern solution to an overheated economy in 1991, which caused voters to feel that he might not be the prime minister we had to have.

Ridgie-didge: genuine.

Rort: fake, cheat: 'He's rorting the voting figures.'

Sheila: woman.

Shonky: unreliable in business: 'He's a bit of a shonk.'

Shout: to buy a round of drinks.

Sickie: a day off work for illness (not necessarily genuine).

Skerrick: a tiny bit: 'There's not a skerrick of evidence for that.'

Skite: boast.

Slag off: to rubbish, criticise, insult, badmouth. In sport, it's called 'sledging'.

Smart alec: a pretentious person who shows off knowledge.

Sook: whinger.

Squatter: a rich farmer. Excessive rural influence on government indicates a 'squattocracy'.

Strine: the language we speak in Straya, as defined in the 1966 book *Let Stalk Strine* by Afferbeck Lauder (actually the linguist Alastair Morrison).

Stubbies: small bottles of beer or a small pair of shorts.

Swim between the flags: what you must do at a beach where the lifesavers have checked for rips and undertows. Also a metaphor for Australia's national identity, somewhere between Britain, America and Asia.

Trendie: an inner city person who frequents the latest restaurants, bars and fashion stores.

Veg out: to relax.

Uey: u-turn: 'Chuck a uey at the lights.'

Walkabout: to wander off, disappear: going walkabout is supposedly a habit of Aboriginal people.

Wanker: a self-indulgent or pretentious or overly intellectual person.

Westie: a person from the working-class suburbs of Sydney or Melbourne.

Whinger: complainer.

Wog: a non-English-speaking immigrant. The term has now been embraced by the children of immigrants, used in such satirical stage shows as *Wogs Out of Work*. Wog kids may call Anglo kids 'skips' (from 'Skippy' the bush kangaroo); originally an illness: 'I got a tummy wog'.

Woop-woop: a mythical village in the outback, beyond the black stump, in the never-never.

Wowser: a prude who tries to stop others having fun.

Write-off: destroyed, tired out: 'After the party, my car was a write-off and so was I.'

Wuss: a wimp, or nervous nellie.

Yabbie*: a small freshwater crayfish found in country ponds and dams; also called 'marron', 'red claw' and 'lobbie'.

Yobbo: an ocker slob.

Zed: the vanishing pronunciation of the last letter of the alphabet. Most Australians under the age of 20 prefer the American 'zee', thus endangering the old Aussie synonym for sleeping — 'putting some zeds in the air'.

Firsts

The Alexander technique

A method of relieving stress by improving posture, developed in Melbourne in the 1890s by Frederick Alexander.

Antivenenes for snake and spider bites

Since the 1950s, scientists at the Commonwealth Serum Laboratories have developed treatments for the bites of the taipan, the brown snake, the death adder, the seasnake, the redback spider and the sea wasp. In 1981, a team led by Struan Sutherland developed an antivenene for funnel-web spider bites.

Aspro

In 1915, George Nicholas, a Melbourne pharmacist, concocted a purer form of aspirin, originally made by the German company Bayer, and it became the world's favourite painkiller.

Bionic ear

In 1978, Graeme Clark of the Royal Victorian Eye and Ear Hospital in Melbourne developed a 'cochlear implant' that alleviates deafness by using a tiny radio to deliver sound directly to the brain.

Black box flight recorder

In 1954, David Warren of the Aeronautical Research Laboratories in Melbourne made a recording device for flight data and cockpit conversations that would be durable enough to survive a plane crash. The modern version is usually coloured orange.

Blue heelers

In 1890, the Australian cattle dog was perfected in Muswellbrook, New South Wales, after years of mixing Scotch collie, dingo, dalmatian and kelpie. It is the only purpose-bred cattle dog in the world.

Boomerang

The name comes from the language of the Turuwal people, who lived just south of Sydney, but the inventor of the wooden club that returns when thrown is unknown.

Call girls

In 1891, Melbourne brothel owners set up the first system of ordering prostitutes by phone.

Cloud seeding

In 1947, the world's first man-made rainstorm soaked Bathurst, New South Wales, after dry ice was sprayed into clouds. The CSIRO Division of Cloud Physics continues to experiment with rainmaking using silver iodide particles around which ice crystals form.

Controlled crying

In the mid-1970s, Christopher Green of the Child Development Unit at the Royal Alexandra Hospital in Sydney introduced a procedure for creating regular sleep patterns in babies. It involves parents letting their child cry for increasingly longer periods before comforting them.

Counterfeit-proof money

In 1988, the Reserve Bank and the CSIRO introduced the world's first banknotes made of polymer plastic, lasting ten times longer than paper notes and almost impossible to forge. The Reserve's company, Securency, now makes money for 23 other countries, from Bangladesh to Zambia.

Dynamic Lifter

In 1971, Norman Jennings of Sydney demonstrated a method of making fertiliser pellets from chicken manure. It is now used around the world.

The Esky

In 1952, the Malley company introduced a portable drink cooler in the form of a steel box within a steel box (with ice between), changing in the 1970s to plastic and increasing the size.

The Fairlight Computer Music Instrument

In 1979, two Sydney engineers, Peter Vogel and Kim Ryrie, invented a music synthesiser that provided a lush backing for such 1980s performers as Peter Gabriel, Kate Bush, Duran Duran, Todd Rundgren and Stevie Wonder.

The feature film

In 1906, the world's first movie to run for more than an hour was *The Story of the Kelly Gang*, made in Victoria by Charles Tait.

Flight across the Pacific Ocean

In 1928, Charles Kingsford Smith was the first to fly from Oakland, California to Brisbane, Queensland.

Forensic lights

In 1989, Ron Warrender and Milutin Stoilovic of the Australian National University in Canberra developed a portable light that shows up invisible clues like blood stains, fingerprints and scribbled-over writing. The Polilight is used by police in 40 countries.

Freestyle swimming

From 1902, the stroke originally known as the Australian Crawl was introduced to the world in touring displays by the Sydney endurance swimmers Syd and Charles Cavill, and became the standard in international competitions.

Granny Smith apples

In 1868, Maria Ann Smith cultivated a long-lasting green apple in her garden in Eastwood, Sydney. Her children marketed it to the world.

Harmful effects of thalidomide

In 1961, William McBride of Sydney revealed that the morning sickness drug, thalidomide, could cause deformities in babies.

The Hawke olive harvester

In 2002, Tony Hawke, a farmer from Wauchope, New South Wales, designed a self-propelled machine that pulls olives off trees without bruising the fruit or damaging the branches. Built by his son Scott, the machine saves time and labour for Australia's booming olive oil industry.

The Hills Hoist

In 1946, Lance Hill welded pipes together in his shed in Adelaide and built a rotary clothesline able to be raised with a crank handle and strong enough for a child to swing on. Selling millions, it became the symbol of the suburban backyard.

The Humespun pipe

In 1910, brothers Walter and Ernest Hume of Melbourne patented a method of making strong pipes by spinning wet concrete inside a mould. By the 1920s, the method was used around the world.

Immunology

Since the Nobel Prize-winning work of Macfarlane Burnet in the 1940s, Australian medical researchers have led the world in helping the body's immune system fight disease. In 1991, Donald Metcalf of the Walter and Eliza Hall Institute in Melbourne identified 'colony stimulating factors' which encourage the body to make white blood cells.

The inflatable escape slide

In 1965, Jack Grant of Qantas invented a slide that helps passengers evacuate a crashed plane and turns into a life raft if the crash is in water.

The Interscan landing guidance system

In 1971, the CSIRO's Paul Wild perfected the ideas of Brian O'Keeffe for using microwave beams to scan the ground and let planes approach runways at a steeper angle.

The irrigation machine

In 1891, George Chaffey started pumping water from the Murray River onto land at Mildura, Victoria, using a massive steam engine he had designed. It turned Mildura into a fruit exporting centre.

Juvenile Court

In 1890, the world's first closed court designed to protect young defendants from 'criminal taint' was set up in Adelaide.

Kelpies

In the 1860s, the first purpose-built sheepdog was bred from Scottish prick-eared collies on Geralda Station near Forbes, New South Wales, and exported to the world after 1872, when it won the first Australian sheepdog trials.

Kiwi boot polish

In 1906, William Ramsay and Hamilton McKellan of Melbourne launched a shoe cream able to restore colour to faded leather. They named it for Ramsay's wife, who was a New Zealander, and by 1920 they had sold 30 million tins around the world. It is now owned by America's Sara Lee corporation.

Letter sorting machine

In 1930, the world's first letter sorter, designed by A.B. Corbett, was installed at the Sydney GPO.

Lithium

In 1949, John Cade, of Melbourne's Royal Park Psychiatric Hospital, started using lithium carbonate to settle the manic side of bipolar disorders.

Microsurgery

Since 1968, the Sydney surgeon Earl Owen has pioneered the use of powerful microscopes to allow the sewing together of separated body parts, especially fingers to hands and hands to arms.

Mulesing sheep

In 1937, the CSIRO recommended a technique developed by the South Australian grazier J.H.W. Mules to remove skin around a sheep's anus where blowflies might lay their eggs. The technique is regarded as cruel by animal liberation groups in the US.

The notepad

In 1902, J.A. Birchall, a stationer in Launceston, Tasmania, first marketed bundles of paper with the sheets gummed together along the top.

The pacemaker

In 1926, Crown Street Women's Hospital, Sydney, developed a machine to keep a baby's heart beating. It evolved into the battery-powered pacemaker made in the US in the 1950s. In the 1970s, the Australian company Telectronics developed a version that could last twenty years.

Pavlova

The weight of evidence now suggests that the recipe for this dessert of meringue, fruit and cream was first published in New Zealand, but it does seem to have been named (after a visiting ballerina) in 1935 by Bert Sachse, the chef at the Esplanade Hotel in Perth.

Pedal wireless

In 1925, Alfred Traeger, an Adelaide engineer, devised a method for rural people without electricity to power radio transmitters by using bicycle pedals attached to a small generator. The invention allowed the Royal Flying Doctor Service to communicate with patients.

Penicillin

In 1940, Howard Florey, an Adelaide scientist working in Oxford, found a way to refine the antibiotic penicillin, then organised its mass production in America.

Permanent pleating

In 1957, the CSIRO released Si-ro-set, a process invented by Arthur Farnsworth for putting creases into wool garments.

Plastic lenses

In 1960, Noel Roscrow set up Scientific Optical Laboratories of Australia in Adelaide to make spectacle lenses out of a plastic called CR39. It became the world's biggest plastic lens maker, and also developed Perma-Gard scratch resistant lens coating and multifocal lenses as an alternative to bifocals.

Preferential voting

Introduced in Queensland in 1892, and in federal elections from 1919, it enables voters to number candidates from most liked to least liked. Combined with compulsory voting (introduced in Queensland in 1915), it makes Australia the most participatory democracy in the world.

Prepaid mail

Before 1838, people paid when a letter was delivered. Then James Raymond, postmaster general of the colony of New South Wales, started selling stamped letter sheets at 15 pence a dozen. Two years later the

London post office introduced the same idea in the form of a penny postage stamp.

Refrigeration

In 1851, James Harrison of Geelong, Victoria, first made artificial ice, using the principle that metal becomes cold when in contact with evaporating ether. His technology was improved in 1861 by Eugene Nicholle of the Sydney Ice Company, who used ammonia in his freezing plants, and was funded by the merchant Thomas Sutcliffe Mort.

Splade

In 1943, William McArthur of Sydney designed a combination knife, fork and spoon marketed to the world in 1962 (as Splayds) by Stokes Pty Ltd.

Stockwhip

Of unknown origin, the kangaroo-hide whip is more than two metres long and controls sheep or cattle by making a cracking noise when it moves faster than the speed of sound.

Stripper harvester

In 1843, near Adelaide, John Bull, a wheat farmer, and John Ridley, a flour miller, developed a machine that pulled the grains from stalks of wheat. It enabled Australia to start exporting wheat to the world.

Stump-jump plough

In 1870, Robert Bowyer Smith of Kalkabury, South Australia, broke a bolt on his plough and found it went over obstacles more easily. His patented version is credited with opening up Australia's scrub to wheat farming.

Surf reel

Designed in 1906 by Lyster Ormsby, captain of the Bondi Lifesaving Club, and built by G.H. Olding, it involved a belt which went around the lifesaver, attached to a rope which went around a giant cotton-reel, by which the lifesaver could be towed back to shore with the person rescued.

Tea tree oil

Originally an Aboriginal medicine, oil distilled from melaleuca leaves can help to relieve cuts, skin infections and acne.

Test-tube babies

Since 1973, Monash University researchers Alan Trounsen, Linda Mohr and Carl Wood have been developing techniques for in-vitro fertilisation. They helped the birth of the world's first test-tube twins in 1983, and the first frozen embryo baby in 1984.

Toilet with dual flush

In 1980, Bruce Thompson, research and development manager with the Caroma company, redesigned the traditional cistern and toilet bowl to allow for two ways of flushing — 11 litres for big jobs and 5.5 litres for small jobs. It can save 32 000 litres of water a year per household.

Totalisator

In 1913, George Julius of Sydney perfected a kind of computer (with wheels, cogs and weights) that automatically recorded bets, displayed odds and calculated winnings to help gambling on horse races. It was bought by racetracks around the world.

Ultrasound

In 1961, George Kossoff and David Robinson of the Commonwealth Acoustic Laboratory in Sydney developed a device for scanning human organs using ultrasonic waves.

Ute

In 1933, Lewis Brandt, chief engineer for Ford in Geelong, Victoria, designed a 'utility vehicle' that combined the seating comfort of a car with the carrying capacity of a small flatbed truck.

Victa mower

In 1952, Mervyn Victor Richardson, a Sydney mechanic, developed a lightweight two-stroke petrol lawnmower, which made his Victa company the biggest mower maker in the world. Slogan: 'Turn grass into lawn'.

Votes for women

South Australia was the second place in the world, after New Zealand, to let women vote in a general election: in 1894. Women voted for the federal government in 1902.

Wine cask

In 1965, Tom Angove of the Angoves wine company in Renmark, South Australia, patented the 'bag in a box' method of packaging and dispensing wine.

Wollemi Pines

In 1994, a park ranger in the Blue Mountains, west of Sydney, stumbled upon a stand of odd-looking conifers that turned out to be the last survivors of the world's oldest plants, unchanged for 200 million years. The Sydney Botanic Gardens Trust managed to breed from the 100 trees in the wild, and now Wollemi Pine seedlings are sold around the world.

Woomera

A breakthrough in weapons technology made more than 10 000 years ago, the woomera, or throwing stick, is a wooden lever that increases the speed and distance a spear will travel. The word comes from the Dharug language used around Sydney Harbour.

Zinc cream

In 1940, the Adelaide branch of Faulding Pharmaceuticals introduced tubes of white zinc oxide cream to block the sun's ultraviolet light and prevent skin cancers. Then, in 1999, Terry Turney, a CSIRO scientist, developed a transparent form of zinc cream.

The most ...

Liked people*

1 **Magda Szubanski**, comedian ('Kath and Kim')
2 **Andrew Denton**, interviewer ('Enough Rope')
3 **Ernie Dingo**, actor/presenter ('The Great Outdoors')
4 **Michael Caton**, actor (*The Castle*, 'Hot Property')
5 **John Wood**, actor ('Blue Heelers')
6 **Bert Newton**, presenter ('Good Morning Australia')
7 **Jamie Durie**, presenter ('Backyard Blitz')
8 **Rove McManus**, comedian/presenter ('Rove Live')
9 **Lisa McCune**, actress ('Blue Heelers', Coles ads)
10 **Sigrid Thornton**, actress ('SeaChange', 'MDA')

*Every six months the research organisation Audience Development Australia shows pictures
of personalities to a sample of 750 viewers in Brisbane, Sydney and Melbourne, and asks how
they feel about the ones they recognise. The above personalities have consistently been most
recognised and liked since 2001.

Prescribed medicines

1 **paracetamol** (pain relief, e.g. Panadol)
2 **amoxicillin** (antibiotic)
3 **salbutamol** (anti-asthma, e.g. Ventolin)
4 **cephalexin** (antibiotic)
5 **temazepam** (sleeping pill, e.g. Normison)
6 **flu virus vaccine**
7 **atorvastatin** (anti-cholesterol)
8 **levonorgestrel/ethinyloestradiol** (contraceptive pill)
9 **diazepam** (tranquilliser, e.g. Valium)
10 **simvastatin** (anti-cholesterol)

Tallest buildings

Sydney Tower (305 metres); **120 Collins Street**, Melbourne (262 metres); **101 Collins Street**, Melbourne (260 metres); **The Rialto**, Melbourne (242 metres); **Chifley Tower**, Sydney (240 metres)

Tallest mountains

Kosciusko (2230 metres above sea level); **Townsend** (2210 metres)

Note: Everest in Asia is 8848 metres

Highest temperature

53.1°C recorded at **Cloncurry**, Queensland, on 16 January 1889

Lowest temperature

-23.0 °C at **Charlotte Pass**, NSW, on 18 June, 1994

Top rainfall

Happy Valley, north Queensland, with 4436 millilitres a year; Australia's average is 465 millilitres, the lowest in the world

Biggest deserts

Great Victoria in Western Australia and South Australia (348 750 square kilometres, or 4.5 per cent of Australia); **Great Sandy** in Western Australia (267 250 square kilometres or 3.5 per cent)

Note: Sahara in Africa is 9 065 000 square kilometres

Game show prize

One million dollars was won by Rob Fulton on *Who Wants To Be A Millionaire* in October 2005. The show went off air in 2006 when host Eddie McGuire became CEO of the Nine network.

Big things

The Big Banana at Coff's Harbour, NSW; **Bull** at Wauchope, NSW; **Trout** at Adaminaby, NSW; **Prawn** at Ballina, NSW; **Cheese** at Bega, NSW; **Merino** at Goulburn, NSW; **Ram** at Wagin, WA; **Crocodile** at Wyndham, WA; **Lobster** at Kingston, SA; **Orange** at Berri, SA; **Ned Kelly** at Glenrowan, VIC; **Penguin** at Penguin, VIC; **Truck** at Dysart, QLD; **Peanut** at Kingaroy, QLD; **Pineapple** at Nambour, QLD; **Guitar** at Tamworth, NSW

World records

The **youngest person to sail solo around the world** is David Griffiths Dicks, who was eighteen when he returned to Fremantle, Western Australia, on 16 November 1996, after 264 days, 16 hours and 49 minutes.

The **oldest continuous circus** in the western world was founded in Launceston in 1852 by Joseph Ashton and is still touring rural Australia with his descendants.

The **highest fee per minute paid to an actor** was US$3.7 million for Nicole Kidman's four-minute commercial for Chanel No. 5 in December 2003.

The **most golf holes** in a day (401) were played by Ian Colston at Bendigo Golf Club, Victoria, on 27 November 1971.

The **heaviest crab** (*Pseudocarcinus gigas*), weighing up to 14 kilograms, is found in Bass Strait near Tasmania.

The **heaviest aircraft ever pulled by a person** was a Boeing 747, weighing 187 tonnes, which was pulled 91 metres in 1 minute 27.7 seconds on 15 October 1997 by David Huxley in Sydney.

The **largest electorate in the world** is Kalgoorlie in Western Australia, which covers 2.6 million square kilometres and stretches 2250 kilometres north to south.

The **largest oyster** (*Ostrea hyotis*), weighing up to 3 kilograms, is found along the Great Barrier Reef in Queensland (which is the world's longest coral reef).

The **largest opal**, weighing 5.27 kilograms, was found at Coober Pedy, South Australia, in 1990.

The **largest wooden building** is Woolloomooloo Bay Wharf, Sydney, built in 1912.

The **largest deposit of iron ore** was discovered in 1952 in Western Australia by Lang Hancock, creating extreme wealth for him and later his wife Rose and his daughter Gina Rinehart.

The **longest train ever assembled**, stretching 7.35 kilometres, took 682 iron ore cars 275 kilometres from BHP's Newman mines to Port Hedland, Western Australia, on 21 June 2001.

The **longest bill** belongs to the Australian pelican, averaging 40 centimetres.

The **longest school lesson** lasted 54 hours, when Murry Burrows taught biology to 26 students at Laidley State High School, Queensland, from 15 to 17 April 2003.

The **largest truffle** outside France, weighing 1 kilogram, was cultivated at Manjimup, Western Australia, in June, 2005.

The **longest earthworm** (*Megascolides australis*), stretching up to 4 metres, is found in Gippsland, Victoria.

The **fastest speed on water** was 511.11 kilometres per hour, achieved by Ken Warby driving the jet-powered hydroplane *Spirit of Australia* on Blowering Dam Lake, New South Wales, on 8 October 1978.

(Source: *Guinness Book of World Records*, 2005)

Icons: physical

The Blue Mountains, west of Sydney
Bondi Beach, Sydney
Broken Hill, NSW
Coober Pedy opal mines, SA
Cradle Mountain National Park, TAS
Daintree Rainforest National Park, north QLD
Dandenong Ranges, north of Melbourne
Federation Square, Melbourne
Flinders Ranges, SA
Fraser Island, north-east of Brisbane
Ghan Railway, 2979 kilometres or 47 hours between Darwin and Adelaide
Great Barrier Reef, 2000 kilometres along QLD coast
Harbour Bridge, Sydney
Indian–Pacific Railway, 4352 kilometres or 67 hours between Sydney
    and Perth
Jenolan Caves, west of Sydney
Kakadu National Park, particularly the Aboriginal rock art at Nourlangie, NT
Kings Canyon, Watarrka National Park, NT
Lord Howe Island, 700 kilometres north-east of Sydney
Margaret River wine region, WA
Melbourne Cricket Ground (also used for football), VIC
Monkey Mia, where dolphins swim close to shore in Shark Bay, WA
National Gallery of Australia, Canberra
Ningaloo coral reef, off WA
Opera House, Sydney
Parliament House, Canberra
Phillip Island, to view the penguin parade, south of VIC
Port Arthur, TAS
South-west Karri forests, WA
Twelve Apostles, rock formations off the Great Ocean Road, VIC
Uluru (Ayers Rock) and **Kata Tjuta** (the Olgas), NT

Icons: cultural

Aboriginal art

A craze started in the 1970s when art dealers discovered the dot paintings of the Pintupi and Luritja people who live at Papunya, 250 kilometres west of Alice Springs, and persuaded them to make more portable creations by using acrylic paints on canvas. The big names are Clifford Possum Tjapaltjarri, who painted vast topographical 'maps' containing dreaming stories, Emily Kngwarreye, who painted the wildflowers and waterholes of the Red Centre, and Rover Thomas, who painted animal stories from the Great Sandy Desert of Western Australia.

Aeroplane Jelly

Coloured sugar and gelatine crystals first sold in 1927 and immortalised by a radio jingle in which a five-year-old girl sang 'I like it for dinner, I like it for tea', because 'a little each day is a good recipe'.

Akubra hats

The best use for the rabbit plague introduced into Australia in 1859. Tasmania's Benjamin Dunkerly turned skins into hats from 1872, naming them after an Aboriginal word for head covering. They're often worn with Drizabones, large oilskin coats designed to cover both horse and rider in a rainstorm.

ANZACs

Originally the acronym for the Australia and New Zealand Army Corps, who landed at Gallipoli in Turkey in 1915 as part of an unsuccessful British plan to stop Turkey's support for Germany in World War I. The word now refers to all servicemen who join the Anzac Day march on 25 April, and has connotations of bravery, loyalty and persistence. Anzac biscuits are made of golden syrup, desiccated coconut, rolled oats, flour, butter and sugar.

Arnott's biscuits

We were upset in 1991 when the American Campbell's company took over the bakery founded in Newcastle in 1865, but we keep eating the Tim Tams, Iced VoVos, Adora Cream Wafers, Saos, Nice, Jatz and Milk Arrowroots.

The Ashes

The prize for victory in cricket tests between England and Australia. The first time we beat England on English soil (1882), the London *Sporting Times* newspaper said English cricket had died and 'the body will be cremated and sent to Australia'. A burnt bail was placed in an urn and given to the Australian team.

Aunty

The Australian Broadcasting Corporation is the government-funded radio, television and web network. Aunty ABC is regarded by some as too artsy-fartsy and lefty-intellectual, and by others as pandering excessively to vulgar tastes, but it is valued for its independence from commercial and political pressures.

Aunty Jack

Played by comedian Grahame Bond, she was the full-bodied trans-gendered bike-riding hero of an ABC comedy series that started in 1972 and generated the hit song ('Farewell Aunty Jack'), a catchphrase ('I'll rip yer bloody arms off') and a more successful spin-off series ('The Norman Gunston Show').

Backyard

That patch of lawn behind the suburban bungalow where Australians enjoy their barbie, their Hill's Hoist and, when they get a pay rise, their swimming pool.

Ben Ean Moselle

The semi-sweet white wine that started Australians on the road to sophistication in the 1960s. Made in Mildura from muscat, gordo and sultana grapes, it offered women an alternative to shandies (beer and lemonade) and sold at the rate of seven million bottles a year by the mid-1970s. The Ben Ean fad was replaced in the 1980s by the chardonnay fad.

Blinky Bill

A cartoon koala created in 1933 by Dorothy Wall in her book *Blinky Bill The Quaint Little Australian* and turned into a TV series in the 1970s.

Blue singlet

Until the 1970s, this was the standard garb of labourers, usually worn with shorts called Stubbies.

Cherry Ripe

Chocolate-coated confection of coconut and cherries introduced in 1924 by MacRobertson's (now owned by Cadbury's).

Chesty Bond

A comic strip hero introduced in 1939 to promote Bond's singlets, of which Australians had bought 300 million by the year 2000.

Chiko Roll

Australia's fast food before America gave us the Big Mac, KFC and Pizza Hut. In 1951, inspired by the Chinese spring roll, Frank McEnroe wrapped a cylinder of dough around minced cabbage, carrot, meat and rice. Deep fried and served with tomato sauce, the rolls were a hit on Frank's snack cart in rural Victoria, so in 1956 he set up a factory in Melbourne to mass produce and freeze them.

Cicadas

Noisy insects that remind us of summer nights.

Cleo

Launched in 1972, and soon selling 200 000 copies a month, it was the first Australian women's magazine to publish nude male centrefolds and to specialise in advice on how to achieve orgasm.

Dad and Dave

Rural characters from an 1899 book called *On Our Selection* by Steele Rudd (real name Arthur Hoey Davis). Dave is dumb, Dad is cunning and Dave's wife Mabel is sweet. John Howard is a fan.

Edna Everage

The sharp-tongued housewife from Moonee Ponds, Melbourne, created in 1955 by Barry Humphries. She has become an international superstar.

Grange Hermitage

Australia's greatest (and most expensive) red wine, created in 1951 by Adelaide wine maker Max Schubert using shiraz grapes with a little cabernet sauvignon. In the 1990s Grange became such a threat to the French wine industry that they made Penfold's remove the word 'hermitage' from the label.

Norman Gunston

The Wollongong dork created for 'The Aunty Jack Show' by actor Garry McDonald. Throughout the late 1970s Gunston managed to host his own successful tonight show whereon he sang, danced and conducted bizarre interviews with unsuspecting celebrities. An attempt to revive Gunston in 1993 ended when McDonald had a nervous breakdown.

Holden cars

The 'all-Australian car' designed by America's General Motors and first built here in 1948. Most nostalgia attaches to the Kingswood in the 1970s and the Commodore in the 1990s.

Barry Jones

A Melbourne schoolteacher with a photographic memory who won a fortune in prizes on the TV quiz show 'Pick-a-Box' in the 1960s and went on to become Minister for Science in the Labor government of Bob Hawke in the 1980s. He symbolised the lovable brain whose ideas are not necessarily practical.

Kath and Kim

The suburban mother and daughter from the ABC's hit sitcom are the Edna Everages of the 21st century. They introduced the catchphrases 'Look at moyee' and 'It's noice, it's different, it's unusual'.

Ned Kelly

A horse thief, bank robber, bushranger and murderer who operated in Victoria's Glenrowan area in the 1870s. He became a legend because he politicised his crimes as part of a struggle between poor Irish peasants and rich English landlords. He was hanged in Melbourne on 11 November 1880. Sidney Nolan's paintings of him in a rectangular black helmet hang in the National Gallery in Canberra.

Lamington

A cube of sponge coated with chocolate and dipped in dried coconut, symbolic of what our grandmothers used to make for afternoon tea.

The loud shirt

In the mid-1980s, Dare Jennings, founder of the Mambo line of surf clothing, commissioned a group of cartoonists to design Hawaiian shirts that would be uniquely Australian. The result was a set of garish parodies of Australian stereotypes. The biggest sellers were 'The Beer Tree' and 'Aussie Jesus' by Reg Mombassa.

Louie the Fly

A dark character created in 1957 by Bryce Courtenay for Mortein fly spray commercials. He apparently has the power to resurrect from the dead — or the spray doesn't work.

The Magic Pudding

A literary character that turned into a metaphor. Created in 1918 by the artist Norman Lindsay, the pudding was a curmudgeon who demanded to be eaten, because 'the more you eats, the more you gets: cut and come again is his name and cut and come again is his nature'. Can the same be said of Australia's natural resources?

Ern Malley

A fictitious poet created in 1944 as a hoax by two real poets, Hal Stewart and James McAuley. They persuaded a literary magazine called *Angry Penguins* to publish Malley's series 'The Darkening Ecliptic'.

Barry McKenzie

The hero of a 1960s comic strip by Barry Humphries in London's *Private Eye* magazine, later made into two movies. The strip satirised how the British saw Australian tourists: as sex-obsessed beer addicts with fifty synonyms for vomiting.

Ginger Meggs

A red-haired larrikin kid in a newspaper comic strip created in 1921 by Jim Bancks.

The Melbourne Cup

Since 1861, the nation has stopped on the first Tuesday afternoon of November to learn which big horse can gallop fastest round the 3200-metre circuit at Flemington racecourse.

Molly Meldrum

As host of the ABC pop music show 'Countdown' between 1974 and 1987, he pioneered an inarticulate interviewing style that amazed and amused the nation. He continues to perfect this style with variety show appearances, wearing a cowboy hat.

Bert Newton

Originally the straight man to Graham Kennedy, he has used his wit, his roundness and his orange hairpiece to charm audiences via the Logie Awards, TV commercials, the daily shopping show 'Good Morning Australia' and, in 2006, the daily game show 'Bert's Family Feud'.

Phar Lap

A big New Zealand-born chestnut gelding who won the Melbourne Cup in 1930, and died suddenly after he started winning races in America. Jealous Americans were suspected of his murder; now it seems he was accidentally poisoned when his trainer Tommy Woodcock gave him an arsenic-based tonic. Phar Lap's stuffed skin is in the Melbourne Museum.

Roy and H.G.

Roy Slaven and H.G. Nelson are mythical sports commentators originally created for radio Triple J by the comedians John Doyle and Greig Pickhaver. They enlivened the television coverage of the last three Olympic Games and have hosted numerous variety shows.

Snugglepot and Cuddlepie

Gumnut babies created in the 1920s by the children's book illustrator May Gibbs. These chubby elves were friendly with native animals and curious about human beings, but lived in fear of the Big Bad Banksia Men. Gibbs also wrote a newspaper comic strip in which she called them Bib and Bub.

Southerly buster

The east coast name for a wind that suddenly cools the city after a humid summer day, known in Perth as the Fremantle Doctor.

Violet Crumble bar

A chocolate-coated honeycomb confection introduced in 1923 by Hoadley's of Melbourne, now owned by Nestlé.

R.M. Williams

Reginald Murray Williams started making saddles, boots, pants and jackets in the north of South Australia in 1934, and in the 1980s his durable garments became a fad with urbanites and tourists. In 1988, he set up the Stockman's Hall of Fame in Longreach, Queensland.

Wogs Out of Work

Satirical stage show launched in 1987 by Nick Giannopoulos, Simon Palomares and Mary Coustas. Gave a comic voice to the children of a million Greek immigrants who had arrived since 1946, and generated the TV series 'Acropolis Now' and the movie *The Wog Boy*.

Created there, embraced here

Abba

Australians bought more of this quartet's albums than any other country (apart from Sweden). We put them on the soundtrack of two of our most successful movies — *Priscilla, Queen of the Desert* and *Muriel's Wedding*. And we formed a tribute band, Bjorn Again, which we exported back to the northern hemisphere.

Big Brother

Long after Americans, British and European TV viewers had lost interest in the idea of observing extroverts trapped in a house, the Australian edition was still rating in the top ten.

Bikini

Invented in 1946 by a Frenchman and named after an atoll where the first US atomic tests were conducted, it first appeared on Aussie beaches in the late 1940s and caused inspectors to escort ladies off the sand to prevent public offence. The first Australian-designed bikini, by Paula Stafford, went on sale at Surfers Paradise in 1952.

Cappuccino

Italians only drink it with breakfast, but Australians drink it all day, frothy or flattened into caffé latte.

Desperate Housewives

During 2005, one in seven Australians watched this dramedy every week, compared with one in 13 Americans. Its suburban glamour and black humour struck a chord in the most suburbanised nation on earth.

Nutella

The chocolate-hazelnut spread created by Pietro Ferrero in Alba, Italy, in 1946 is Australia's second best-selling spread (after Vegemite).

The Phantom

Invented by American Lee Falk in 1936, but barely remembered in his homeland, the 'Ghost Who Walks', with his wolf Hero, his horse Devil and his support team the pygmy Bandar, became immortal here as a magazine and newspaper comic strip.

Poker machines

Invented in America in 1908, but redesigned by Sydney's Len Ainsworth in the 1950s, slot machines were legalised for use in clubs by the New South Wales Government in 1956. Now Australia has 180 000 of them — 21 per cent of the world's total — and we put through $80 billion a year, winning back $70 billion.

Thongs

Australia must admit that New Zealand gave the world the rubber sandal with the band between the first and second toe, allegedly based on ancient Japanese footwear. The Kiwis call them 'jandals', while the Americans call them 'flip-flops' (and use the word 'thong' for what we call a 'g-string'). Our athletes rode a giant thong in the 2000 Olympics opening ceremony, and costume designer Lizzie Gardiner made a dress entirely of pink thongs for Hugo Weaving in the 1994 film *Priscilla, Queen of the Desert*. Overpriced thongs are now called Havianas.

Weber portable barbecue

Introduced here in 1978 by American entrepreneur Ross McDonald, this pod-shaped miracle allowed apartment dwellers to join a fad once confined to the backyard.

Made here, embraced there

Bananas in Pyjamas
The giant yellow do-gooders of Cuddles Avenue, originally created for
'Play School' in 1988, now do marketing magic for the ABC in sixty
countries.

Fosters beer
Invented in Victoria in 1887, now bottled in nine countries and sold in 150,
Fosters has its fan base in Britain, where they imagine it's Australia's top-
selling beer (a title actually held by Victoria Bitter).

Kangaroo as a delicacy
Most Australians avoid eating kangaroo meat, possibly because of its
associations with our TV friend Skippy, but it is consumed eagerly by the
French and the Germans, who consider it a health food with low fat, high
protein and plenty of iron.

Matrix series and Star Wars trilogy
These were largely filmed in Sydney, with Australians in all the bit parts.

Neighbours
The Melbourne teen soap and its Sydney clone 'Home and Away' are seen
in fifty countries by people who envy our big houses, white teeth and
sunny lifestyle.

Paddle Pop
Invented in 1953 by Edwin Street at the Corrimal Ice Works, south of
Sydney, and now owned by the English company Unilever, the ice-block is
a hit in eighteen countries, including Vietnam and China.

Speedos
First made in 1929 by Sydney's MacRae Knitting Mills, and best known
for the men's tight 'budgie smugglers' introduced in 1961, they became the
cossie of choice for all 52 countries competing in the swimming events of
the Montreal Olympics in 1976. Now the company is American-owned.

Ugg boots

The sheepskin slippers developed in the 1960s to keep the feet of Sydney surfers warm are a fad with US entertainers. An American company claimed ownership of the name in 2003, but in January 2006 the Australian trademark regulator ruled that Ugg, or Ugh (short for ugly), was a generic name (like thongs) and could be used by anybody.

The Wiggles

Created in 1991 for an ABC pre-schooler's program, the singing comedians Greg, Murray, Anthony and Jeff in their colourful skivvies earn around $45 million a year by selling products in America and franchising their concept to non-English speaking countries. In 2005, they were named 'Australian exporter of the year' for selling 17 million DVDs and videos.

Mysteries

What happened to Azaria Chamberlain?

In 1980, a two-month-old girl disappeared from a tent in a camping ground near Uluru. Her mother, Lindy Chamberlain, said she must have been dragged away by a dingo. In 1982, Mrs Chamberlain was convicted of the child's murder and spent four years in gaol before being declared innocent.

Who put the dope in Schappelle Corby's bag?

In 2005, a 28-year-old Queensland woman, described as a 'beauty student', was arrested at Denpasar Airport in Bali after customs officers found a four-kilogram package of cannabis in her boogie-board bag. After trial, she was sentenced to twenty years in gaol. She says she was the victim of an international smuggling racket. Conspiracy theories flourish about Australian airport baggage handlers, drug dealers and even members of her family.

Where is the Tasmanian tiger?

The last known thylacine died in Hobart Zoo in 1936, but Tasmanians occasionally report forest sightings of a wolf-like creature with yellow fur and dark stripes on its back.

What happened to Harold Holt?

In December 1967, the prime minister disappeared while swimming in rough seas at Cheviot Beach, south of Melbourne. One entertaining theory held that he was picked up by a Chinese submarine. Another held that Holt was depressed over waning support for his commitment to the Vietnam War.

Who carved the Marree Man?

In 1988, a four-kilometre-long carving of an Aboriginal hunter appeared in the desert sands of Lake Eyre South, sixty kilometres from the town of Marree in South Australia. In order to create the landmark, the site must have been surveyed from space and the figure would have taken months to plough.

What killed Bogle and Chandler?

On New Year's Day, 1963, the bodies of Gilbert Bogle, a CSIRO scientist, and Margaret Chandler, the wife of another CSIRO scientist, were found on the banks of the Lane Cove River near Chatswood Golf Course in Sydney. No cause of death has been determined. There was speculation they were working on secret drug projects for the CIA.

Who was attacking the Family Court?

In 1980, Judge David Opas of the Family Court was shot dead at the front door of his Sydney home. In 1984, a bomb went off at the Family Court in Parramatta, Sydney, and later that year the wife of Family Court judge Ray Watson was killed by a bomb at their home. No one has been charged with these crimes.

Where did all the money go?

During the 1980s, Australians briefly abandoned their traditional scepticism about tall poppies and admired the entrepreneurs Alan Bond (then boss of Channel 9 and Castlemaine Tooheys brewery), Christopher Skase (the boss of Channel 7 and Mirage Resorts) and John Elliott (boss of Elders IXL food company and Carlton United brewery).

By the mid-1990s, Bond and Skase were bankrupt, accused of fraud and with debts in the billions. And by the early 2000s, Elliott, a Liberal Party president once touted as a potential prime minister, was bankrupt and under investigation by the National Crimes Authority.

Our faith in capitalism was also shaken by the collapse in 2001 of One.Tel, a communications company founded by Jodee Rich with a $375 million investment from James Packer (now Australia's richest man) and a $575 million investment from Lachlan Murdoch (the son of one of the world's richest men).

These collapses would surely be candidates for the title of Australia's biggest corporate fiasco, but they were overshadowed by the collapse of the insurance company HIH in 2001, with debts totalling $5.3 billion. CEO, Ray Williams, and a director, Rodney Adler, were sentenced to four years gaol, and businessman Brad Cooper got eight years for bribing HIH staff.

Economists like to say that money is never lost: it simply moves around. So where is it?

Creatures we love

Budgerigar: mini-parrot which became the world's most popular caged bird after the naturalist John Gould took a breeding pair back to England in 1840

Dingo: wolf-like wild dog brought here 7000 years ago by Aboriginal immigrants

Echidna: monotreme (using the same hole for excretion, sex and egg laying) with sharp spines, long snout and sticky tongue for catching insects; its image is on our five cent coin

Emu: big flightless bird bred for meat, oil and feathers; less flavoursome than kangaroo, best eaten as mince or prosciutto

Frill neck lizard: harmless reptile that puffs out its collar to frighten predators

Galah: a noisy parrot usually with a pink head and grey back

Kangaroo: hopping marsupial that carries its young in a pouch; its image is on our one dollar coin; estimated population: 40 million; its meat is high in iron and low in fat, best cooked on a barbecue

Koala: tree-climbing marsupial that eats eucalyptus leaves; currently endangered by the disease chlamydia; not edible

Kookaburra: kingfisher bird that comes in two types, the laughing jackass and the howling jackass

Platypus: improbable furry duck-billed swimming mammal which is also a monotreme; its image is on our twenty cent coin

Wombat: marsupial like a small furry pig that lives in a burrow

Creatures we hate

Bluebottle: stinging nuisance that regularly invades beaches

Bulldog ant: most dangerous ant in the world, up to four centimetres long, with an occasionally fatal sting

Cane toad: imported nuisance that kills native animals in northern regions

Crown of Thorns starfish: slowly consuming the coral of the Great Barrier Reef

Parasitic bush tick: world's most infectious blood feeder

Saltwater crocodile: up to eight metres long and found in swamps and rivers near the northern coastline; partial to foolish tourists

Sea wasp (or box jellyfish): the sting can kill; most often found in northern tropical waters between October and May

Sharks, especially the white pointer, the whaler and the tiger: they kill or injure an average of four swimmers a year

Snakes, especially the taipan, the tiger and the death adder: each year they kill three people who don't receive antivenene in time

Spiders, especially the funnel-web and the redback: deaths are now rare because of antivenene

Creatures in danger of extinction

Allan's lerista (reptile)
Bare rumped sheathtail bat
Galaxias (fish)
Long footed potoroo
Loggerhead turtle
Northern bettong
Red-finned blue-eye (fish)
Red-tailed phascogale (mouse)
Southern cassowary
Western swamp tortoise
White bellied frog

Since 1788, seventeen of Australia's 270 species of mammals, three of the 700 species of birds, four of the 200 species of frogs and 61 of the 15 000 species of flowering plants **have become extinct**.

Creatures renamed
(by the CSIRO to make them more lovable)

The rabbit-eared bandicoot became the bilby
Dusky hopping mouse: wilkinti
Western chestnut mouse: moolpoo
Water rat: rakali
Greater stick-nest rat: wopilkara
Plains rat: palyoora
Brush tailed rabbit rat: pakooma
Black footed tree rat: djintamoonga
Bush rat: mootit
Long haired rat: mayaroo

Changes

Is life in Australia getting better, getting better all the time? A Bureau of Statistics report called *Measures of Australia's Progress 2006* shows we're richer, healthier and better educated than we were ten years ago, but we're poisoning our air, salting our soil and endangering our animals. The following were the main qualities of life measures that changed in a decade.

Health: Life expectancy is three years longer than it was in the mid-90s. But in 2005, 11 per cent of Australians reported having serious 'mental or behavioural problems', compared with 6 per cent in 1995.

Training: The proportion of adults with vocational or higher education rose from 46 per cent to 58 per cent. But Canada, Japan and New Zealand have higher proportions.

Income: Real net national disposable income grew by 3 per cent a year over the decade, and the unemployment rate dropped from 9 per cent to 5 per cent. We spend our new wealth on entertaining ourselves. In the mid 1990s, the average Australian spent $2549 a year on food and $1919 on recreation and culture; in the mid noughties the figures are $2784 on food and $3079 on recreation.

Crime: The prevalence rates for victims of personal crimes (such as assault and robbery) between 1998 and 2005 showed an increase from 4.8 to 5.3 per cent.

Environment: Over the decade, the number of terrestrial bird and mammal species thought to be extinct, endangered or vulnerable rose from 120 to 169, an increase of 41 per cent; total net greenhouse emissions rose by 8.8 per cent; and 46 500 square kilometers of agricultural land 'were assessed as having a high salinity hazard'. Australia had, in 2003, 'the highest net per capita level of greenhouse gas emissions of OECD countries (27.5 tonnes). Sweden had the lowest per capita emissions (5.5 tonnes).' Now that's a serious contribution to climate change.

Heavy dates

New Year's Day: public holiday on 1 January (or nearest weekday)

Australia Day: public holiday on 26 January (or nearest weekday)

Chinese New Year: first week of February

Sydney Gay and Lesbian Mardi Gras: last weekend in February

Labour Day: public holiday on 7 March in Western Australia, 14 March in Victoria and Tasmania, 2 May in Queensland, and 3 October in New South Wales, the ACT and South Australia

Daylight saving: (except in Queensland and Western Australia) clocks go back one hour on the last Sunday in March, and forward one hour on the last Sunday in October

Good Friday and Easter Monday: public holidays in late March or early April

April Fool's Day: hoaxes permitted till midday on 1 April

Anzac Day: public holiday on 25 April (or nearest weekday)

Mother's Day: second Sunday in May

Adelaide Cup Day: public holiday on 16 May in South Australia

Foundation Day: public holiday on 6 June in Western Australia

The Monarch's birthday: public holiday on 13 June in all States except Western Australia, where it falls on 26 September

Father's Day: first Sunday in September

Melbourne Cup Day: public holiday in Victoria on the first Tuesday in November

Remembrance Day: 11 November — a minute's silence at 11 a.m. to mark the end of World War I

Christmas Day: public holiday on 25 December (or nearest weekday)

Boxing Day: public holiday on 26 December, Sydney to Hobart Yacht Race begins

Proclamation Day: public holiday in South Australia on 27 December

4

IT'S BEEN SAID OF US ...

Australia's most inspiring speeches

Arthur Phillip, the first governor of the colony of New South Wales, warning the convict-settlers that he was about to get tough on **law and order**, 7 February 1788:

'Should I continue to pass by your enormity with an ill-judged and ill-bestowed lenity, the consequence would be, to preserve the peace and safety of the settlement, some of the more deserving of you must suffer with the rest, who might otherwise have shewn themselves orderly and useful members of our community. Therefore you have my sacred word of honour that whenever ye commit a fault, you shall be punished, and most severely. Lenity has been tried. To give it further trial would be vain. I am no stranger to the use you make of every indulgence. I speak of what comes under my particular observation: and again I add that a vigorous execution of the law (whatever it may cost my feeling) shall follow closely upon the heels of every offender.'

Robert Lyon, a teacher of Greek and English, at a public meeting at Guildford in Sydney in June 1833, discussing how **Aboriginal people** might react to white settlers:

'The law of nations will bear them out in repelling force by force. They did not go to the British Isles to make war upon you; but ye came from the British Isles to make war upon them. Ye are the invaders of their country, ye destroy the natural productions of the soil on which they live, ye devour their fish and their game, and ye drive them from the abodes of their ancestors … They have all along shown themselves ready to be reconciled, desirous to live in peace and amity with you, and even willing to be taught your manners, laws, and polity. Choose for yourselves. If ye determine upon a war of extermination, civilised nations will be mute with astonishment at the madness of a policy so uncalled for, so demoniacal. When your doom is passed, your own children, for whose sakes ye have invaded the country, will join with the disinherited offspring of those ye have slain to pour a flood of curses upon your memory.'

Richard Windeyer, a lawyer born in England, at the inaugural meeting of the Aborigines Protection Society in October 1838, discussing **the rights of Aboriginal people**:

'I cannot look upon the natives as the exclusive proprietors of the soil; nor can I entertain the ridiculous notion that we have no right to be here. I view colonisation on the basis of the broad principle laid down by the first and great Legislator in the command He issued to man "to multiply and replenish the Earth". The hunting propensities of the natives cause them to occupy a much larger portion of land than would be necessary to their support if it were under cultivation. And the only way to make them cultivate it is to deprive them of a considerable portion of it. The natives have no right to the land. The land, in fact, belongs to him who cultivates it first.'

Robert Lowe, a lawyer and member of the Legislative Council, at a protest meeting of 5000 people at Circular Quay on 11 June 1849, demanding an end to the **transportation of convicts** to provide cheap labour for landowners:

'The stately presence of our city, the beautiful waters of our harbour, are this day again polluted with the presence of that floating hell: a convict ship … I view this attempt to inflict the worst and most degrading slavery on the colony only as sequence of that oppressive tyranny which has confiscated the lands of the colony for the benefit of a class. That class has felt our power: they are not content to get the lands alone, which without labour are worthless, and therefore they must enrich themselves with slaves. As in America, oppression was the parent of independence, so it will be in this colony. And so, sure as the seed will grow into the plant, and the plant to the tree, in all times, and in all nations, so will injustice and tyranny ripen into rebellion, and rebellion into independence.'

Ned Kelly, a bushranger, explaining why he **killed policemen**, while holding hostages in a bank in Jerilderie in New South Wales on 10 February 1879:

'Certainly their wives and children are to be pitied, but they must remember those men came into the bush with the intention of scattering pieces of me and my brother all over the bush, and yet they know and acknowledge I have been wronged and my mother and four or five men lagged innocent. And is my brothers and sisters and my mother not to be pitied also, who has no alternative, only to put up with the brutal and cowardly conduct of a parcel of big, ugly, fat-necked, wombat-headed, big-bellied, magpie-legged, narrow-hipped, splay-footed sons of Irish bailiffs or English landlords which is better known as officers of Justice or Victorian Police, who some calls honest gentlemen … A Policeman is a disgrace to his country, not alone to the mother that suckled him. In the first place he is a rogue in his heart, but too cowardly to follow it up without having the Force to disguise it. Next, he is a traitor to his country, ancestors and religion, as they were all Catholics before the Saxons and Cranmore yoke held sway. Since then they were persecuted, massacred, thrown into martyrdom and tortured beyond the ideas of the present generation.'

Louisa Lawson, the publisher of *The Republican* newspaper (assisted by her son Henry), speaking at the inaugural meeting of the Dawn Club on 23 May 1889, demanding the **vote for women**:

'Pray why should one half of the world govern the other half? Is it just to first ensure the silence of the weaker half by depriving them of a citizen's status, and then inform them that by the laws of the stronger section this is the way they must act and this is the way the world may legally use them? Here in New South Wales every man may vote, let his character be bad, his judgement purchasable, and his intellect of the weakest, but an honourable and thoughtful and good woman may be laughed at by such men: they can carry what laws they please in spite of her. In divorce, men are protected from infidelity: not women. Wives may still be forced to live in the same house with a husband whom they hate and fear. Have women no need of a vote to protect them in these things and in the multitude of other interests affecting women and children? It remains for the women of Australia to say how long they will lag in the rear of the great onward march of liberal thought and women's advances. We have examples. Now we only need our own efforts.'

Henry Parkes, the premier of New South Wales, addressing the Federation Conference (he was called 'the father of federation' but died four years before it was achieved) in Melbourne on 6 February 1890, urging the **colonies to unite**:

'The crimson thread of kinship runs through us all. We know we represent a race for the purpose of settling new colonies which never had its equal on the face of the earth. We know, too, that conquering wild territory and planting civilised communities therein, is a far nobler, more immortalising achievement than conquest by feats of arms. Is there a man living in any part of Australasia who will say that it would be to the advantage of the world that we should remain disunited, with our animosities, border customs and all the frictions which our border customs tend to produce, till the end of time? I do not believe there is a sane man in the whole population who will say such a daringly absurd thing. As separate colonies we are of little consequence, but the potentate does not exist, the ruling authority in human affairs does not exist, who would lightly consider the decision of a united Australasia. We should grow at once: in a day, as it were: from a group of disunited communities into one solid, powerful, rich and widely respected power.'

Alfred Deakin, the first attorney-general of Australia (he was prime minister from 1903 to 1910), introducing the *Immigration Restriction Act* on 12 September 1901:

'It is not the bad qualities but the good qualities of these alien races that make them dangerous to us. It is their inexhaustible energy, their power of applying themselves to new tasks, their endurance and low standard of living that makes them such competitors. The effect of the contact of two peoples, such as our own and those constituting the alien races, is not to lift them up to our standard, but to drag our labouring population down to theirs … Members on both sides of the house and of all sections of all parties: those in office and those out of office: with the people behind them, are all united in the unalterable resolve that the Commonwealth of Australia shall mean a "white Australia", and that from now henceforward all alien elements within it shall be diminished. We are united in the resolve that that this Commonwealth shall be established on the firm foundation of unity of race, so as to enable it to fulfil the promise of its founders, and enjoy to the fullest extent the charter of liberty under the Crown which we now cherish.'

John Monash, commander of Australian forces on the Western Front in World War I, explaining why we should celebrate **Anzac Day**, 25 April 1927:

'Anzac Day makes a special appeal to the hearts of all of us because of the special place it holds in our history, for it was on this day 12 years ago that the flower of Australia's youth flung itself against the beetling cliffs of Gallipoli and performed a memorable feat of arms which instantly welded the people of Australia into a nation, and proved to the entire world that our men and women were not unworthy of their sires. It is not too much that the people should pause for one day in the year to do homage to those men and to keep alive the spirit which animated that host of departed friends. But our duty does not end there. On us who have survived the stress of war and who have been safely restored to our homeland is laid the duty of helping to restore to Australia the mighty loss of that legion of men by devoting our lives and energies to that class of nation building in which they would have shared had they been spared. Remember, in war those who came out of battle had to carry on the fight in reduced numbers, so we who have been fortunate enough by the blessing of Providence to survive the war must now do our part, but not only our part; we must take up the burden of those we left behind. Only so can we worthily honour their memory.'

Jack Lang, the premier of New South Wales, trying to **open the Sydney Harbour Bridge** on 19 March 1932 (before Lang could cut the ribbon, Francis de Groot, a member of a right wing group called The New Guard, rode up and slashed the ribbon with his sword, saying, 'On behalf of decent and loyal citizens of New South Wales, I now declare this bridge open'):

'The achievement of this bridge is symbolical of the things Australians strive for, but have not yet attained. The bridge itself unites people who have similar ideals and aims, but are divided by physical and geographical boundaries. Just as Sydney has completed the material bridge that will unite her people, so will Australia ultimately perfect the bridge which it commenced 30 years ago. The statesmen of that period set out to build a bridge of common understanding, that would serve the whole of the people of our great continent. The builders of that bridge, as the builders of this bridge, meet with disappointments, which make the task difficult sometimes: often delicate. But that bridge of understanding among the Australian people will yet be built, and will carry her on to that glorious destination which every man who loves our native land feels is in store for her.'

Robert Menzies, an opposition backbencher in the process of forming the Liberal Party, discussing '**the forgotten people**' in federal parliament on 22 May 1942:

'We don't have classes here as in England, and therefore the terms don't mean the same. It is necessary, therefore, that I should define what I mean when I use the expression "the middle class": those people who are constantly in danger of being ground between the upper and nether millstones of the false class war; the middle class who, properly regarded, represent the backbone of this country … First it has a stake in the country. It has responsibility for homes: homes material, homes human, homes spiritual … Second, the middle class, more than any other, provides the intelligent ambition which is the motive power of human progress … Third, the middle class provides more than any other the intellectual life which marks us off from the beast; the life which finds room for literature, for the arts, for science, for medicine and the law … Individual enterprise must drive us forward. That doesn't mean that we are to return to the old and selfish notions of laissez-faire. The functions of the state will be more than merely keeping the ring within which the competitors will fight. Our social and industrial obligations will be increased. There will be more law, not less; more control, not less. But what really happens to us will depend on how many people we have who are of the great and sober and dynamic middle class: the strivers, the planners, the ambitious ones. We shall destroy them at our peril.'

Ben Chifley, prime minister from 1945 to 1949, explaining **the priorities of the Labor Party** on 12 June 1949:

'I try to think of the Labor movement, not as putting an extra sixpence into somebody's pocket, or making somebody prime minister or premier, but as a movement bringing something better to the people, better standards of living, greater happiness to the mass of the people. We have a great objective: the light on the hill: which we aim to reach by working for the betterment of mankind not only here but anywhere we may give a helping hand. If it were not for that, the Labor movement would not be worth fighting for. If the movement can make someone more comfortable, give to some father or mother a greater feeling of security for their children, a feeling that if a depression comes there will be work, that the government is striving its hardest to do its best, then the Labor movement will be completely justified.'

William McKell, premier of New South Wales from 1941 to 1947 and governor-general of Australia from 1947 to 1953, supporting Australia's 'populate or perish' **immigration program**, 22 January 1951:

'The great immigration project upon which we are now firmly embarked is undoubtedly one of the most constructive and notable events in the history of Australia. Immigration means the development of our resources, the strengthening of our security and defences and the rapid expansion of our population, while to hundreds of thousands of people in the United Kingdom and Europe, it means the opportunity to live a new life in Australia ... In the nineteenth century period of rapid growth, a sense of "mateship", fair play, independence of spirit and self-reliance was engendered which forms a vital part of our tradition of nationhood. It is these qualities, which are among the best in the Australian character, that we must seek to pass on to the newcomers. By a wise handling of assimilation, our migrants will not only conform to our standards of citizenship, but will add their own contribution. There will be give and take. Assimilation will be a two way process, demanding much of both migrants and ourselves, and the result will be mutual enrichment. For the migrants are bringing to Australia not only the benefits of their knowledge and skills, but of their age-old cultures. The old and new should blend into a better and more varied community of people.'

Robert Menzies, prime minister of Australia from 1949 to 1966, welcoming **Queen Elizabeth II** to Australia, 18 February 1963:

'It is a proud thought for us to have you here, to remind ourselves that in this great structure of government which has evolved, you, if I may use the expression, are the living and lovely centre of our enduring allegiance ... You will be seen in the next few weeks by hundreds of thousands, and I hope by millions, of Australian subjects. This must be to you now something that is almost a task. All I ask you to remember in this country of yours is that every man, woman and child who even sees you with a passing glimpse as you go by will remember it, remember it with joy, remember it in the words of the old seventeenth century poet who wrote those famous words: "I did but see her passing by, but yet I love her till I die."'

Arthur Calwell, leader of the opposition in federal parliament from 1960 to 1967, opposing the government's decision to send troops to **join America's forces in Vietnam**, 4 May 1965:

'We do not think it is a wise decision. We do not think it is a timely decision. We do not think it will help the fight against communism. On the contrary, we believe it will harm that fight in the long term. We do not believe it will promote the welfare of the people of Vietnam. On the contrary, we believe it will prolong and deepen the suffering of that unhappy people so that Australia's very name may become a term of reproach among them … And may I, through you, Mr Speaker, address this message to the members of my own Party … I offer you the probability that you will be traduced, that your motives will be misrepresented, that your patriotism will be impugned, that your courage will be called into question. But I also offer you the sure and certain knowledge that you will be vindicated; that generations to come will record with gratitude that when a reckless government wilfully endangered the security of this nation, the voice of the Australian Labor Party was heard, strong and clear, on the side of sanity and in the cause of humanity and in the interests of Australia's security.'

Harold Holt, prime minister of Australia from 1966 to 1967, explaining Australia's **support for the Vietnam War** to US President Lyndon Baines Johnson, 30 June 1966:

'You have in us not merely an understanding friend but one staunch in the belief of the need for our presence with you in Vietnam. We are not there because of our friendship, we are there because, like you, we believe it is right to be there and, like you, we shall stay there as long as seems necessary to achieve the purposes of the South Vietnamese government and the purposes that we join in formulating and progressing together. And so, sir, in the lonelier and perhaps even disheartening moments which come to any national leader, I hope there will be a corner of your mind and heart which takes cheer from the fact that you have an admiring friend, a staunch friend that will be All The Way With LBJ.'

Robin Boyd, an architect and author of *The Australian Ugliness*, delivering the Boyer Lecture on ABC radio on 17 October 1967, with the theme **'creative man in a frontier society'**:

'Australia is divided: not into halves, but into two uneven sections: by a jagged vertical crack near the left end. Facing each other across it are two Australians who are as different and wary of each other as the Aborigine and Captain Cook. On the larger side is the modern Australian who believes in the long established, still popular anti-intellectual Australian values, who is convinced that the Australian state and rate of progress are satisfactory. On the other is the modern Australian who sees so many shortcomings in Australian social development that he is on the point of despair. The evolution from a sponge-like culture, absorbing everything useful that floats by, to a crawling and finally free-ranging active culture happens spontaneously and quite suddenly in a society, but only when enough individuals consciously revolt against being sponges ... In the ever more crowded and competitive world of the last third of the twentieth century the product that the whole world is craving, and will reward most highly whenever it finds it, is not our wool, and not even our iron or bauxite or natural gas that lay here so long waiting to be discovered. It is brains: not just acquisitive brains and not just academic brains, but creative brains, imaginative brains exercised to the edge of their capacity: which is the sort of exercise that has been least respected in our 180 years of development.'

Germaine Greer, touring Australia to promote her book, *The Female Eunuch*, explaining the advantages of **women's liberation**, March 1972:

'It's not at all alien to the Australian character. It's not at all alien to Australian women, who are probably in some ways less bullshit-ridden than other women. And they know something about hard work, most of them, if only because the garden is so hard to handle and it's got funnel webs in it. Women's liberation is sexy, it's exciting, it's all kinds of things, and it's here to stay. There is no turning it back. A radicalised woman is not able to go back to the old one-two hanky dropping routine. It's just too nauseating.'

Don Dunstan, premier of South Australia from 1967 to 1968 and from 1970 to 1979, moving for the **decriminalisation of homosexuality**, 18 October 1972:

'It is certainly contrary to the majority public taste. But surely that is not sufficient for us to say that, because most of us do not regard this as something that is in any way attractive but rather, repulsive, other people who view the matter differently should have our views imposed on them privately. The second suggestion is that there is a necessity to help the people involved. The law as it stands does not help the people involved: it does not assist people to seek help. What is more, of course, one must face the fact that the majority of people who are homosexual do not regard homosexuality as a disease at all, nor do they regard it as a condition to be cured. They regard it as natural and normal. In those circumstances, I do not believe that society has any right whatever to trespass in this area. The purpose of the criminal law is to protect persons from physical harm and from active affront, and their property from harm also. Outside of that area, I believe that the criminal law has no place at all, and it is for the social influences of the community to impose or induce or persuade the moral standards which various sections of the community advocate, to establish the moral standards which will be accepted by the majority. The law is not a means of enforcing morality.'

Gough Whitlam, prime minister from 1972 to 1975, opening **Labor's election campaign**, 13 November 1972:

'Men and women of Australia. The decision we will make for our country on the second of December is a choice between the past and the future, between the habits and fears of the past, and the demands and opportunities of the future. There are moments in history when the whole fate and future of nations can be decided by a single decision.

For Australia, this is such a time. It's time for a new team, a new program, a new drive for equality of opportunities. It's time to create new opportunities for Australians, time for a new vision of what we can achieve in this generation for our nation and the region in which we live.'

Frank Sinatra, visiting singer, discusses **the media** while addressing his audience in Melbourne's Festival Hall, 8 July 1974 (the speech resulted in union members from all industries refusing to serve him for the remainder of his tour):

'We have a name in the States for their counterparts. They're called parasites, because they take and take and take and never give, absolutely never give. I don't care what you think about any press in the world. I say they're bums and they're always gonna be bums, every one of them. There are just a few exceptions to the rule: some good editorial writers who don't go out in the street and chase people round. It's the scandal man that really bugs you, drives you crazy. It's two-bit type work that they do. They're pimps, they're just crazy. And the broads who work in the press are the hookers of the press. Need I explain that to you? I might offer them a buck and a half, I'm not sure. I once gave a chick in Washington two dollars, and I overpaid her, I found out.'

Gough Whitlam, reacting to **the dismissal** of his government, 11 November 1975 (Labor lost the ensuing election):

'Ladies and gentlemen. Well may we say "God Save the Queen", because nothing will save the Governor-General. The proclamation which you have just heard read by the Governor-General's secretary was countersigned Malcolm Fraser, who will undoubtedly go down in Australian history from Remembrance Day 1975, as Kerr's cur. They won't silence the outskirts of Parliament House, even if the inside has been silenced for the next few weeks … Maintain your rage and enthusiasm through the campaign for the election now to be held and until polling day.'

Malcolm Fraser, prime minister from 1975 to 1983, addressing the Liberal Federal Council in July 1981, explains a **puritan philosophy** often attributed to him:

'Over the years, a quotation about what life was or wasn't meant to be like has often been talked about. Some people have said it represents my philosophy. I think that now is the time to let you into a secret. Only half of the quotation is ever quoted. In full, it says: Life is not meant to be easy, my child; but take courage, it can be delightful.'

Paul Keating, prime minister from 1992 to 1996, launching the Year of the World's **Indigenous People**, at Redfern Park, Sydney, 10 December 1992:

'We took the traditional lands and smashed the traditional way of life. We brought the diseases. The alcohol. We committed the murders. We took the children from their mothers. We practised discrimination and exclusion. It was our ignorance and our prejudice. And our failure to imagine these things being done to us. With some noble exceptions, we failed to make the most basic human response and enter into their hearts and minds. We failed to ask: How would I feel if this were done to me? As a consequence, we failed to see that what we were doing degraded all of us … And if we have a sense of justice, as well as commonsense, we will forge a new partnership. Ever so gradually, we are learning how to see Australia through Aboriginal eyes, beginning to see the wisdom contained in their epic story. I think we are beginning to see how much we owe the Indigenous Australians and how much we have lost by living so apart.'

Paul Keating, thanking election workers, 13 March 1993:

'Well, this is the sweetest victory of all. This is the victory for the true believers, the people who in difficult times have kept the faith. And to the Australian people going through hard times: it makes their act of faith all that much greater. It will be a long time before an Opposition party tries to divide this country again. It will be a long time before somebody tries to put one group of Australians over here and another group over there. The public of Australia are too decent and they are too conscientious and they are too interested in their country to wear those sorts of things. This I think has been very much a victory of Australian values, because it was Australian values on the line and the Liberal Party wanted to change Australia from the country it had become, a cooperative, decent, nice place to live where people have regard for one another … The people of Australia have taken us on trust and we'll return that trust and we'll care about those people out there, particularly the unemployed: we want to get them back to work. If we can't get them back to work immediately, as sure as hell we are going to look after them. We are not going to leave them in the lurch and we are going to put our hand out and we are going to pull them up behind us. And we are going to move along, this country is going to move along together.'

Poppy King, a businesswoman in the cosmetics industry, making the **case for a republic** at the Constitutional Convention in Canberra, 10 February 1998:

'If I had to explain to someone who had lost their memory that Australia's head of state was not actually Australian, I would feel utterly ridiculous. Take away the historical connection and the concept is absurd. No one is asking this nation to lose its collective memory nor to deny the importance of Britain in our history. What we are asking is to examine our future, to explore our values and reassess whether our current Constitution reflects those. It seems that a main argument against Australia becoming a republic is a fear of change, a desire to maintain the status quo rather than take the risk to develop something better. This desire concerns me greatly. Think of all the developments that have improved our lives, both tangibly and intangibly, that would have been lost had this attitude prevailed. Apathy is the enemy of progress and progress requires change. I believe that Australia is one of the greatest democracies in the world. I believe that it is us as Australians that can take the credit for our harmonious society, not the Constitution itself. Becoming a republic is one enormous national pat on the back. Generations of Australians past and present have created a fantastic country, but it is not from the wording of our Constitution, however good those words may be, but from the way we as citizens put these words into practice. Many say the change to a republic is purely symbolic. If this is the case, let me pose this question with all due respect: why keep this particular symbol? You may say because of a special bond that we have with Britain, a bond that I am sure is a lot more meaningful to many of my elders than is possible for me to understand. I am here to listen to their views and I respect their passion, but I would like to ask them this: how do we explain to future generations that we place our faith in a citizen of a country other than our own? How do we explain to them that no matter how hard they work they can never be part of a monarchy? How do I explain to the children that I may have one day that they have been lucky enough to be born into a country where anything — anything — is possible except to become our head of state?'

John Carroll, Professor of Sociology at La Trobe University in Melbourne, delivering the Deakin lecture on 12 May 2001, explaining **'the dreaming' of white Australians**:

'A people, to feel free to let their character virtues speak unimpeded, must be at ease in themselves. One of the leading symptoms of insecurity is a tendency to extremism, to fanaticism or fundamentalism. Peoples, like individuals, take flight into ideology, dogmatism and ranting when they feel under inner threat. It is a leading mark of Australia as a political culture to have always and without exception been sceptical of idealism, hostile to extremists, innately drawn to the moderate, the sensible, the unassuming. It points to a fundamental security of being. Special warmth has grown for kangaroo, koala, platypus and echidna that is more than the cuddly toy sort. The marsupials set a tone, in their way of being. In part it is their lack of aggression: except when cornered. The quiet way they go about negotiating their habitat has affinity with the way the people respond to bureaucratic controls. Calm resistance, except when cornered, has met the Australia Card, Byzantine new tax systems and grand attempts to tidy up the constitution. The kookaburra reminds humans, prone to taking themselves seriously, that they are easy to laugh at. The totemism of Aboriginal tribal culture seems to be colonising the colonisers.'

John Howard, prime minister from 1996, addressing the memorial service for victims of the **Bali bombings**, 17 October 2002:

'Our nation has been changed by this event. Perhaps we may not be so carefree as we have been in the past, but we will never lose our openness, our sense of adventure. The young of Australia will always travel. They will always reach out to the young of other nations. They will always be open, fun loving, decent men and women … It will take a long time for these foul deeds to be seen in any kind of context. They can never be excused. Australia has been affected very deeply, but the Australian spirit has not been broken. The Australian spirit will remain strong and free and open and tolerant. I know that is what all of those who lost their lives would have wanted and I know it is what all of those who grieve for them would want.'

Steve Vidler, actor (*Two Hands*) and director (*Blackrock*), explains why Australians prefer **American-made movies** to locally-made ones, 11 April 2005:

'A contributing factor is the power of the national myth, both American and Australian. The American myth is the myth of their nation's settlement — that an individual with strong character can undertake a daunting task, overcome seemingly insurmountable odds, and become a great success. The Australian myth is also based on our nation's settlement — that we are convicts, delinquents, struggling outsiders, persecuted by an uncaring and alien authority, trapped in a harsh environment we did not choose and do not understand, that all survival and validation relies on not rising above or separating from the group, failure and suffering are our lot, and the best we can hope for is to survive. US films represent their myth with great commercial success. It is a very palatable story and one most audience members would prefer to see on a Friday night after a hard week at work. Australian films represent their myth equally well [*Gallipoli*, *Lantana* and *Shine* exemplify the dramatic version, *The Castle* and *Muriel's Wedding* the comic] but it is a far less palatable myth, and commercially far less saleable.

Sometimes we try to appropriate the American myth for our stories. And a strange thing happens. Mostly Australian audiences will not believe it. Our myth [itself a fanciful construct with little relation to the realities of our history] is so deeply ingrained that we distrust any narrative that sees our environment as essentially benign, or triumphant success as the deserved outcome of our struggle. But we will willingly believe these things of Americans. Or of Australians pretending to be Americans. To this problem there is no solution but time. I believe future generations will outgrow the convict/bushranger/Anzac myth, and embrace a new narrative that reflects more accurately the enormous potential that lies within them and within this blessed and beautiful country.'

5

THE THINGS
WE LIKE

Favourite flicks

The films seen by the greatest number of living Australians, based on box office earnings adjusted for changing admission prices, are:

1 **The Sound of Music** (1965) 'There is nothing more irresistible to a man than a woman who's in love with him.'

2 **Crocodile Dundee** (1986) 'That's not a knife. THAT'S a knife ... Just kids having fun.'

3 **Dr Zhivago** (1966) 'You lay life on a table and cut out all the tumours of injustice. Marvellous.'

4 **Titanic** (1997) 'You must do me this honour, Rose. Promise me you'll survive. That you won't give up, no matter what happens, no matter how hopeless. Promise me now, Rose, and never let go of that promise.'

5 **Star Wars** (1977) 'The Force is what gives a Jedi his power. It's an energy field created by all living things. It surrounds us and penetrates us. It binds the galaxy together.'

6 **E.T.** (1982) 'I'll be right here.'

7 **Shrek 2** (2004) 'Thank you, gentlemen. Someday I will repay you, unless of course I can't find you, or if I forget.'

8 **Lord of the Rings: The Return of the King** (2003) 'The man who can wield the power of this sword can summon to him an army more deadly than any that walks this earth. Put aside the ranger. Become who you were born to be.'

9 **Babe** (1995) 'Baa-ram-ewe, baa-ram-ewe. To your breed, your fleece, your clan be true.'

10 **Jaws** (1975) 'We're gonna need a bigger boat.'

11 **Grease** (1978) 'I just had the best summer of my life and now I have to go. It isn't fair.'

12 **The Man from Snowy River** (1982) 'Male company will be a pleasant relief in this hothouse of female emotions.'

13 **Lord of the Rings: Fellowship of the Ring** (2001) 'One ring to rule them all. One ring to find them. One ring to bring them all and in the darkness bind them.'

14 **Jurassic Park** (1993) 'God creates dinosaurs. God destroys dinosaurs. God creates man. Man destroys God. Man creates dinosaurs.'

15 **Pretty Woman** (1990) 'I appreciate this whole seduction thing you've got going on here, but let me give you a tip: I'm a sure thing.'

16 **Lord of the Rings: The Two Towers** (2002) 'Where is it? Where is it? They stole it from us, our precious. Curse them! We hates them! It's ours it is, and we wants it!'

17 **The Sting** (1974) 'Aren't you gonna stick around for your share?'
'Nah, I'd only blow it.'

18 **Harry Potter and the Philosopher's Stone** (2001) 'You're a little scary sometimes, you know that. Brilliant. But scary.'

19 **The Lion King** (1993) 'Look inside yourself, Simba. You are more than what you have become. You must take your place in the Circle of Life.'

20 **Star Wars Episode 1: The Phantom Menace** (1999) 'There was no father. I carried him, I gave birth, I raised him. I can't explain what happened.'

21 **Ryan's Daughter** (1971) 'I can wait till they burn it out.'

22 **Forrest Gump** (1994) 'He may be the stupidest son of a bitch, but damn, he sure is fast!'

23 **A Clockwork Orange** (1972) 'That was a real kick and good for laughs and lashings of the old ultraviolence.'

24 **The Godfather** (1972) 'My father made him an offer he couldn't refuse.'

25 **Finding Nemo** (2003) 'I don't know where I am . . . I don't know what's going on. I think I lost somebody but I, I can't remember.'

26 **Harry Potter and the Chamber of Secrets** (2002) 'Dobby is very sorry, Dobby had to iron his hands.'

27 **Crocodile Dundee 2** (1988) 'Tell Mick if he wants his clothes back, he can fetch them his bloody self.'

28 **The Towering Inferno** (1975) 'You know we got lucky tonight — body count's less then 200. Someday you're gonna kill ten thousand in one of these firetraps.'

29 **Mrs Doubtfire** (1993) 'My first day as a woman and I am already having hot flushes.'

30 **Independence Day** (1996) 'I'm just a little anxious to get up there and whup E.T.'s ass.'

Money-making Australian films

1 **Crocodile Dundee** (1986), box office total $48 million
2 **Babe** (1995), $37 million
3 **Moulin Rouge** (2001), $28 million
4 **Crocodile Dundee II** (1988), $25 million
5 **Strictly Ballroom** (1992), $22 million
6 **The Dish** (2000), $18 million
7 **The Man from Snowy River** (1982), $17 million
8 **The Adventures of Priscilla, Queen of the Desert** (1994), $16 million
9 **Muriel's Wedding** (1994), $16 million
10 **Young Einstein** (1988), $13 million
11 **Lantana** (2001), $12 million
12 **Gallipoli** (1981), $12 million
13 **The Wog Boy** (2000), $12 million
14 **The Piano** (1993), $11 million
15 **Mad Max II** (1981), $11 million
16 **The Castle** (1997), $10 million
17 **Shine** (1996), $10 million
18 **Phar Lap** (1983), $9 million
19 **Crackerjack** (2002), $9 million
20 **The Man Who Sued God** (2001), $8.5 million
21 **Ned Kelly** (2003), $8 million
22 **Looking For Alibrandi** (2000), $8 million
23 **Babe 2: Pig in the City** (1998), $8 million
24 **Crocodile Dundee in LA** (2001), $8 million
25 **Rabbit-Proof Fence** (2002), $7.5 million

Australian movies' **share of total box office**: 10 per cent in 1977; 16 per cent in 1982; 24 per cent in 1986; 10 per cent in 1994; 8 per cent in 2000; 1.3 per cent in 2004; 3 per cent in 2005 (top film *Wolf Creek*, with $6 million).

Source: MPDAA and AFC

Top telly

The most watched programs of all time

1 **Diana Spencer's funeral** (channels 9, 7, 10, ABC), 1997
2 **Olympic opening and closing ceremonies** (7), 2000
3 **Wedding of Charles and Diana** (9, 7, 10, ABC), 1981
4 **Cathy Freeman's Olympic gold run** (7), 2000
5 **Olympic swimming events** (7), 2000
6 **Tennis: Australian Open final** (7), 2005
7 **Rugby World Cup final** (7), 2003
8 **Australian Idol final verdict** (10), 2004
9 **Olympics opening ceremony** (10), 1984
10 **The Sound of Music**, first TV showing (9), 1977
11 **Commonwealth Games opening ceremony** (9) 2006
12 **The Block auction** (9), 2003
13 **11 September reportage on 12 September** (9, 7, ABC), 2001
14 **Boxing: Rose v Rudkin** (10), 1969
15 **The World Of The Seekers** (9), 1968
16 **Roots mini-series** (10), 1977
17 **Moon landing** (9, 7, 10, ABC), 1969
18 **AFL Grand Final** (10), 1996
19 **Big Brother winner announced** (10), 2004
20 **AFL Grand Final** (7), 2005
21 **The National IQ Test** (9), 2002
22 **World Cup Soccer Final** (9), 2002
23 **The Beatles sing for Shell** (9), 1964
24 **Raiders of the Lost Ark** (10), 1985
25 **Homicide** (7), 1972

Source: OZTAM and ACNielsen

Most successful
Australian series

1 **Homicide**, Melbourne cop drama (7), 1964–75
2 **Blue Heelers**, drama about cops in rural Victoria (7), 1994–2006
3 **The Secret Life Of Us**, gritty soap (10), 2001–04
4 **The Mavis Bramston Show**, satirical sketch series (7), 1964–68
5 **SeaChange**, adult comedy soap (ABC), 1998–2000
6 **Water Rats**, Sydney cop drama (9), 1996–2001
7 **McLeod's Daughters**, rural soap (9), 2001–
8 **The Comedy Company**, sketches (10), 1988–91
9 **Home and Away**, teen soap (7), 1988–
10 **The Norman Gunston Show**, comedy/chat (ABC and 7), 1975–79
11 **Neighbours**, teen soap (7 and 10), 1985–
12 **Hey Dad**, family sitcom (7), 1984–94
13 **Frontline**, media satire (ABC), 1994–97
14 **A Country Practice**, rural soap (7), 1981–93
15 **Kath and Kim**, satirical sitcom (ABC), 2001–
16 **The Paul Hogan Show**, sketches (7 and 9), 1973–82
17 **Prisoner**, crime soap (10), 1979–87
18 **Number 96**, sexy soap (10), 1972–77
19 **Mother and Son**, family sitcom (ABC), 1984–94
20 **Division 4**, suburban cop drama (9), 1969–74
21 **Play School**, toddler entertainment (ABC), 1966–
22 **All Saints**, hospital drama (7), 1998–
23 **Hey, Hey It's Saturday**, variety (9), 1971–99
24 **Border Security**, documentary about customs (7), 2004–
25 **Dancing with the Stars**, talent quest (7), 2005–

Audience share of Australian networks in 2005: Channel 9 about 23 per cent;
Channel 7, 22 per cent; Channel 10, 19 per cent; ABC, 14 per cent;
SBS, 4 per cent; All pay channels, 16 per cent.

Top-selling DVDs of all time

1 **Finding Nemo** (2004)
2 **Shrek 2** (2004)
3 **Monsters Inc** (2002)
4 **The Two Towers** (2003)
5. **Harry Potter and the Prisoner of Azkaban** (2004)
6 **Harry Potter and the Chamber of Secrets** (2003)
7 **Fellowship of the Ring** (2002)
8 **The Fast and the Furious** (2005)
9 **Pirates of the Caribbean** (2004)
10 **Return of the King** (2004)
11 **Ice Age** (2002)
12 **Harry Potter and the Philosopher's Stone** (2002)
13 **Gladiator** (2000)
14 **Lion King** (2004)
15 **Shrek** (2001)
16 **Spider-Man** (2002)
17 **Star Wars II: Attack of the Clones** (2002)
18 **Madagascar** (2005)
19 **Matrix** (1999)
20 **The Incredibles** (2005)
21 **Harry Potter and the Goblet of Fire** (2006)
22 **Troy** (2004)
23 **Grease** (2002)
24 **Matrix Reloaded** (2003)
25 **Dances With Wolves** (2001)

Source: GFK Marketing

Amount Australians spent on **buying DVDs** in 2005: $975 million.

Amount spent on **cinema tickets** in 2005: $818 million.

Mighty music

Top selling CDs since 1986

1 **Whispering Jack**, John Farnham*
2 **Come On Over**, Shania Twain
3 **Jagged Little Pill**, Alanis Morissette
4 **Innocent Eyes**, Delta Goodrem*
5 **Thriller**, Michael Jackson
6 **Savage Garden**, Savage Garden*
7 **Falling Into You**, Celine Dion
8 **Abba Gold**, Abba
9 **Immaculate Collection**, Madonna
10 **Recurring Dream**, Crowded House*
11 **Rumours**, Fleetwood Mac
12 **Chisel**, Cold Chisel*
13 **Soul Deep**, Jimmy Barnes*
14 **Come Away With Me**, Norah Jones
15 **1**, The Beatles
16 **Forgiven Not Forgotten**, The Corrs
17 **Get Born**, Jet*
18 **Greatest Hits Collection**, Queen
19 **Grease** (film soundtrack)
20 **The Sound of White**, Missy Higgins*

*Australian made

Source: Australian Record Industry Association. CDs replaced vinyl recordings around 1985 and exact sales figures before that year are lost in the mists of time. This explains the absence of big sellers from the 1960s and 1970s, such as Elton John, The Rolling Stones, Neil Diamond, Billy Joel, Paul McCartney, Pink Floyd, The Bee Gees and Dire Straits.

ARIA Hall of Fame

Peter Allen, pop singer/composer ('I Still Call Australia Home'), 1960s–92

Angels, rock band ('Take a Long Line'), 1970s–80s

Australian Crawl, rock band ('Boys Light Up'), 1980s

Jimmy Barnes, rock singer ('Working Class Man'), 1980s–

The Bee Gees, pop group ('Spicks and Specks'), 1960s–90s

Graeme Bell, jazz bandleader and pianist ('Bull Ant Blues'), 1940s–90s

Don Burrows, jazz bandleader and flute, clarinet and sax, 1960s–80s

Cold Chisel, rock band ('Khe Sanh'), 1970s–80s

Richard Clapton, pop singer ('Girls on the Avenue'), 1960s–90s

Smoky Dawson, country singer ('Never Been to Gundagai'), 1950s–90s

Daddy Cool, rock'n'roll band ('Eagle Rock'), 1970–75

Horrie Dargie, bandleader and harmonica player ('Green Door'), 1950s–99

Divinyls, punk and rock band ('I Touch Myself'), 1981–90s

Slim Dusty, country singer ('Pub with No Beer'), 1950s–90s

The Easybeats, pop band ('Friday on my Mind'), 1960s

John Farnham, pop singer ('You're the Voice'), 1960s–90s

Renee Geyer, pop/jazz singer ('Say I Love You'), 1970s–90s

Percy Grainger, classical composer and pianist ('English Country Garden'), 1920s–61

Hunters and Collectors, rock band ('Talking to a Stranger'), 1980s–90s

Icehouse, technorock band ('Great Southern Land'), 1977–90s

INXS, rock band ('Need You Tonight'), 1980s–

Col Joye, pop singer ('Be Bop A Lula'), 1950s–60s

Paul Kelly, rock/folk singer and composer ('To Her Door'), 1980s–90s

Jimmy Little, country singer ('Royal Telephone'), 1960s

Little River Band, pop band ('Reminiscing'), 1970s–90s

Masters Apprentices, rock band ('Poor Boy'), 1960s–70s

Men At Work, pop band ('Land Down Under'), 1970s–80s

Olivia Newton-John, pop singer ('Physical'), 1960s–90s

Johnny O'Keefe, rock singer ('Shout'), 1950s–78

Normie Rowe, pop singer ('Shakin' all Over'), 1960s

The Saints, punk band ('I'm Stranded'), 1970s–80s

The Seekers, pop group ('Georgie Girl'), 1960s–70s

Sherbet, pop band ('Howzat'), 1970s–80s

Glenn Shorrock, pop singer ('Help Is on Its Way'), 1960s–90s

Skyhooks, pop band ('Living in the Seventies'), 1970s–80s

Split Enz, pop band ('I Got You'), 1970s–80s

Joan Sutherland, opera singer ('Lucia di Lammermoor'), 1960s–80s

Billy Thorpe, rock singer ('Most People I Know Think That I'm Crazy'), 1960s–90s

Harry Vanda and **George Young**, pop composers ('Love Is In The Air'), 1960s–90s

Ross Wilson, pop singer and composer ('Daddy Cool'), 1960s–80s

Three Australian compositions appear in the list of '500 Most Influential Rock Songs of All Time' issued by the Rock and Roll Hall of Fame in Cleveland, Ohio: 'Highway to Hell' and 'Back in Black' by **AC/DC**, and 'Beds are Burning' by **Midnight Oil**.

Best songs about us

1 'Down Under', **Men at Work** (1982)

The narrator, a backpacker, finds Australia is so fashionable in Europe that a man in Brussels gave him a Vegemite sandwich. He mocks the stereotype of a land where 'women glow' and 'men chunder'.

2 'Tie Me Kangaroo Down, Sport', **Rolf Harris** (1960)

A dying stockman gives instructions to his friends, such as minding his platypus duck, Bill, tanning his hide when he's died, Clyde, and letting his abos go loose, Bruce.

3 'Waltzing Matilda', **Banjo Paterson** (1895)

A wanderer (swagman) steals a sheep (jumbuck) and, in trying to escape the police (troopers), drowns in a pond (billabong), ultimately returning as a ghost to ask 'Who'll come a waltzing matilda with me?' A matilda is a backpack.

4 'I Still Call Australia Home', **Peter Allen** (1980)

The narrator has been to many exciting places but misses his own country. Sometimes parodied as 'I still call Australia collect', it was adopted as an advertising jingle for Qantas.

5 'The Sounds of Then', **Gangajang** (1985)

The narrator reminisces about sitting on a patio watching the lightning over the cane fields and breathing the humidity. Then he laughs and thinks 'This is Australia'.

6 'Shaddup You Face', **Joe Dolce** (1981)

An immigrant recalls his mother's irritation when he expresses nostalgia for his homeland. She tells him Australia is not so bad, in fact 'it's a-nice-a-place'.

7 'I am (you are, we are) Australian', **Bruce Woodley** and **Dobe Newton** (1987)

The narrator outlines the many different backgrounds of this country's residents — Aboriginal, convict, farmer, immigrant — and concludes that we share a dream and sing with one voice.

8 'The Pub With No Beer', **Gordon Parsons** and **Slim Dusty** (1957)

Various outback characters — stockman, boss, swagman, blacksmith — remark that there is nothing so morbid, lonesome or drear as a bar that can only offer wine and spirits.

9 'Click Go the Shears', **traditional** (1800s)

The narrator tells how an old man beats 'the ringer' (the fastest shearer) in removing the wool from a 'bare bellied ewe', and concludes, 'He works hard, he drinks hard, and goes to hell at last'.

10 'Up There Cazaly', **Mike Brady** (1979)

The song honours Roy Cazaly, a 1930s Melbourne footballer with a talent for leaping. The crowd urges him to fly like an angel and get in there and fight.

11 'Come On Aussie, Come On', **Mojo advertising agency** (1979)

Originally written to promote Channel 9's coverage of cricket in 1979, the song names famous cricketers and boasts of the fitness of the Australian team.

12 'Beds are Burning', **Midnight Oil** (1986)

The narrator argues that it is time to give Aboriginal people their land back, or at least pay rent, because it belongs to them. Midnight Oil's 'The Power and the Passion', discussing whether Australia has too much sun and too much Uncle Sam, could be added to this list as well.

13 'Solid Rock', **Goanna** (1982)

The narrator reminds white Australians they are standing on sacred ground, controlled historically by white man, white law and white gun.

14 'Neighbours', **Jackie Trent** and **Tony Hatch** (1986)

The theme to the television soap suggests that with a little understanding, suburban residents can become friends.

15 'Botany Bay', **traditional** (late 1700s)

With a bizarre chorus of 'tooral-li ooral-li addity', a convicted pickpocket farewells England and anticipates seven years in Sydney. He concludes, 'Come all you young dukies and duchesses, take warning by what I do say. Mind that all is your own as you touchesses, or you'll join us in Botany Bay.'

16 'I've Been Everywhere, Man', **Geoff Mack** (1962)

The narrator boasts of his travel experiences in a list beginning with Tullamore, Seymour, Lismore and Mooloolaba. It was later parodied by Norman Gunston, who listed only Wollongong and Dapto.

17 'True Blue', **John Williamson** (1982)

The narrator wonders what it means to be Australian and whether traditional values, such as standing by a mate, would disappear if they sell us out like sponge cake.

18 'My Island Home', **Neil Murray** (1985)

The narrator, stuck in the desert (or, in the Christine Anu version, the city), recalls growing up by the sea among the salt water people.

19 'Australiana', **Billy Birmingham**, performed by **Austen Tayshus** (1983)

The narrator makes puns of the names of his friends at a party, as in Vegie might; Nulla bores; let's go, Anna; Marie knows; my cossie, Oscar; he'll lead you astray, Leana; and where can Marsu pee, Al?

20 'Skippy The Bush Kangaroo', **Eric Jupp** (1968)

The theme for the television series, it describes the eponymous animal as a true friend.

The [whole] national anthem

Written by Peter Dodds McCormick in 1878 and approved by referendum (against 'Waltzing Matilda' and 'God Save the Queen') in 1977, the anthem was edited down by government officials in 1984 to the two verses in **bold type**. Here's the whole thing:

Australians all let us rejoice,
For we are young and free;
We've golden soil and wealth for toil,
Our home is girt by sea;
Our land abounds in Nature's gifts
Of beauty rich and rare;
In history's page, let every stage
Advance Australia fair!
In joyful strains then let us sing,
'Advance Australia fair!'

When gallant Cook from Albion sail'd,
To trace wide oceans o'er,
True British courage bore him on,
Till he landed on our shore.
Then here he raised Old England's flag,
The standard of the brave;
With all her faults we love her still,
'Britannia rules the wave!'
In joyful strains then let us sing
'Advance Australia fair!'

Beneath our radiant Southern Cross,
We'll toil with hearts and hands;
To make this Commonwealth of ours
Renowned of all the lands;
For those who've come across the seas
We've boundless plains to share;
With courage let us all combine
To advance Australia fair.
In joyful strains then let us sing
'Advance Australia fair!'

While other nations of the globe
Behold us from afar,
We'll rise to high renown and shine
Like our glorious southern star;
From England, Scotia, Erin's Isle,
Who come our lot to share,
Let all combine with heart and hand
To advance Australia fair!
In joyful strains then let us sing
'Advance Australia fair!'

Shou'd foreign foe e'er sight our coast,
Or dare a foot to land,
We'll rouse to arms like sires of yore
To guard our native strand;
Britannia then shall surely know,
Beyond wide ocean's roll,
Her sons in fair Australia's land
Still keep a British soul.
In joyful strains the let us sing
'Advance Australia fair!'

Sporting spectacles

The ones we watch:
(In order of match-attendance and popularity on TV)

1 **AFL** (Australian Football League, aka Aussie Rules, preferred in Victoria, South Australia and Western Australia)
2 **NRL** (National Rugby League, preferred in Queensland and New South Wales)
3 **Cricket**
4 **Tennis**
5 **Horse racing**
6 **Motor sports**
7 **Rugby union**
8 **Basketball**
9 **Soccer**
10 **Netball**

The ones we do:

1 **Walking**: 18 per cent of men walk, 33 per cent of women.
2 **Aerobics/gym**: 9 per cent of men, 13 per cent of women.
3 **Swimming**: 10 per cent of men, 12 per cent of women.
4 **Golf**: 12 per cent of men, 2 per cent of women.
5 **Tennis**: 8 per cent of men, 6 per cent of women.

Players we admire:

Athletics: Betty Cuthbert was our greatest ever runner, winning three gold medals in the 1956 Olympics and another in 1964. Cathy Freeman won the gold medal in the 400 metres race at the 2000 Olympics.

Cricket: Steve Waugh, Australia's most successful captain, played in 164 Tests between 1984 and 2004. Allan Border scored 11 174 runs in 156 Tests between 1978 and 1994. Shane Warne, despite time spent chatting up women, took 620 wickets in 125 Tests between 1991 and 2005. Don Bradman, who retired in 1948 (and died in 2001), averaged 99.94 runs per Test innings.

Cycling: Ryan Bayley won two gold medals for cycling at the 2004 Olympics.

Football: Tony Lockett, playing AFL for St Kilda and for Sydney, has scored the most goals in a career (1360 between 1983 and 2002). Ryan Girdler, playing rugby league for New South Wales, has scored the most points in a State of Origin series (52 points in 2000) and scored the most tries in a match (3) and the most goals in a match (10).

Golf: Greg Norman won the British Open in 1986 and 1993. Karrie Webb won the US Women's Open in 2000 and 2001 and the British Women's Open in 1999 and 2002.

Motor bikes: Mick Doohan won the motorcycle world championships five times between 1994 and 1998.

Motor cars: Jack Brabham won the Formula 1 world car racing championships three times between 1959 and 1966.

Netball: Anne Sargeant played in Australia's world-beating teams in 1979 and 1983 and captained Australia from 1983 to 1987.

Sailing: Kay Cottee was the first woman to sail solo non-stop around the world (in 1988).

Skiing: Michael Milton won four gold medals at the 2002 Winter Paralympics and holds the record as the world's fastest skier on one leg (198.7 kilometres per hour).

Squash: Sarah Fitz-Gerald won the World Open women's squash championships five times between 1996 and 2002.

Surfing: Layne Beachley, who describes herself as 'the most competitive human being on the planet', won the women's world surfing championships six times between 1998 and 2003.

Swimming: Ian Thorpe holds the world records in 200-, 400- and 800-metre freestyle and is a role model for metrosexuality. Dawn Fraser was the first woman to swim 100 metres in less than a minute and won gold medals at the Olympics of 1956, 1960 and 1964. Shane Gould won three gold, one silver and one bronze at the 1972 Olympics.

Tennis: Rod Laver won Wimbledon four times and the Grand Slam (Wimbledon, French Open, Australian Open and US Open) in 1962 and '69. Margaret Court won the women's Grand Slam in 1970.

Triathlon: Brad Beven won the Triathlon World Cup (swim, run, cycle) four times from 1992 to 1995.

Wheelchair racing: Louise Sauvage, whose motto is 'You never know what you can achieve until you try', won gold medals at three Olympic games and the Boston Marathon four times.

In the **2004 Olympics**, Australia won 17 gold medals, placing it number 4 after the US, China and Russia.

What we read

The top-selling books since 1986:

1 **Harry Potter and The Philosopher's Stone**, J.K. Rowling
2 **Harry Potter and the Goblet of Fire**, J.K. Rowling
3 **Harry Potter and the Prisoner of Azkaban**, J.K. Rowling
4 **Harry Potter and the Chamber of Secrets**, J.K. Rowling
5 **The Da Vinci Code**, Dan Brown
6 **Harry Potter and the Order of the Phoenix**, J.K. Rowling
7 **Solomon's Song**, Bryce Courtenay*
8 **The Potato Factory**, Bryce Courtenay*
9 **The Liver Cleansing Diet**, Sandra Cabot*
10 **Angela's Ashes**, Frank McCourt
11 **From Strength to Strength**, Sara Henderson*
12 **The Celestine Prophecy**, James Redfield
13 **Four Fires**, Bryce Courtenay*
14 **The Blue Day Book**, Bradley Trevor Grieve*
15 **Harry Potter and the Half-Blood Prince**, J.K. Rowling
16 **Men Are From Mars, Women Are From Venus**, John Gray
17 **Wild Swans**, Jung Chang
18 **Tommo and Hawk**, Bryce Courtenay*
19 **Matthew Flinders' Cat**, Bryce Courtenay*
20 **Billy**, Pamela Stephenson
21 **The Lord of the Rings**, J.R.R. Tolkien
22 **Your Mortgage and How to Pay it Off in Five Years**, Anita Bell*
23 **Angels and Demons**, Dan Brown
24 **Brother Fish**, Bryce Courtenay*
25 **The Footrot Flats series**, Murray Ball
26 **A Fortunate Life**, A.B. Facey*
27 **Memoirs of a Geisha**, Arthur Golden
28 **Black Notice**, Patricia Cornwell
29 **Bridget Jones' Diary**, Helen Fielding
30 **The Bride Stripped Bare**, Nikki Gemmell*

31 **The CSIRO Total Wellbeing Diet**, Manny Noakes*

32 **Whitethorn**, Bryce Courtenay*

33 **Spycatcher**, Peter Wright*

34 **Wicked**, Morris Gleitzman and Paul Jennings*

35 **Burke's Backyard**, Don Burke*

36 **The Horse Whisperer**, Nicholas Evans

37 **Spotless**, Shannon Lush and Jennifer Fleming*

38 **The Power of One**, Bryce Courtenay*

39 **Life's Little Instruction Book**, H. Jackson Brown Jr

40 **Out of My Comfort Zone**, Steve Waugh*

*Australian

Source: Australian Publishers Association

Peak periodicals:

1 **Sunday Telegraph**, Sydney: 702 000 a week

2 **Sunday Herald Sun**, Melbourne: 623 000 a week

3 **Sunday Mail**, Brisbane: 610 000 a week

4 **Australian Women's Weekly**: 610 000 a month

5 **Herald Sun**, Melbourne: 545 000 a day

6 **Woman's Day**: 526 000 a week

7 **Sun-Herald**, Sydney: 520 000 a week

8 **New Idea**: 432 000 a week

9 **Daily Telegraph**, Sydney: 388 000 a day

10 **West Australian** (Saturday edition), Perth: 380 000 a week

11 **Sydney Morning Herald** (Saturday edition): 365 000 a week

12 **Reader's Digest**: 355 000 a month

13 **Sunday Times**, Perth: 354 000 a week

14 **That's Life**: 346 000 a week

15 **Super Food Ideas**: 341 000 a month

16 **Courier-Mail** (Saturday edition), Brisbane: 327 000 a week

17 **Sunday Mail**, Adelaide: 325 000 a week

18 **Better Homes and Gardens**: 300 000 a month.

19 **Age** (Saturday edition), Melbourne: 300 000 a week

20 **Weekend Australian**: 294 000 a week

Source: Audit Bureau of Circulations

Poems

Some excerpts to get you started …

Bell-birds by Henry Kendall (1869)

By channels of coolness the echoes are calling,
And down the dim gorges I hear the creek falling:
It lives in the mountain where moss and the sedges
Touch with their beauty the banks and the ledges.
Through breaks of the cedar and sycamore bowers
Struggles the light that is love to the flowers;
And, softer than slumber, and sweeter than singing,
The notes of the bell-birds are running and ringing.

The Sentimental Bloke by C.J. Dennis (1915)

'Twas on a Saturdee, in Colluns Street,
An': quite by accident, o'course: we meet.
Me pal 'e trots 'er up an' does the toff:
'E allus wus a bloke fer showin' off.
'This ere's Doreen,' 'e sez. 'This 'ere's the Kid.'
I dips me lid.
'This 'ere's Doreen,' 'e sez. I sez 'Good day.'
An' bli'me, I 'ad nothin' more ter say!
I couldn't speak a word, or meet 'er eye.
Clean done me block! I never been so shy,
Not since I was a tiny little cub,
An' run the rabbit to the corner pub:
Wot time the Summer days wus dry and 'ot:
Fer me ole pot.
Gorstrooth! I seemed to lose me pow'r o' speech.
But 'er! Oh, strike me pink! She is a peach!
The sweetest in the barrer! Spare me days,
I carn't describe that cliner's winnin' ways.
The way she torks! 'Er lips! 'Er eyes! 'Er hair! …
Oh, gimme air!

Freedom on the Wallaby by Henry Lawson (1891)

Australia's a big country
An' Freedom's humping bluey,
An' Freedom's on the wallaby
Oh! Don't you hear 'er cooey?
She's just begun to boomerang,
She'll knock the tyrants silly,
She's goin' to light another fire
And boil another billy.
So we must fly a rebel flag,
As others did before us,
And we must sing a rebel song
And join in rebel chorus.
We'll make the tyrants feel the sting
O' those that they would throttle;
They needn't say the fault is ours
If blood should stain the wattle!

The Magic Pudding by Norman Lindsay (1918)

Politeness be sugared, politeness be hanged,
Politeness be jumbled and tumbled and banged
It's simply a matter of putting on pace,
Politeness has nothing to do with the case.
Eat away, chew away, munch and bolt and guzzle,
Never leave the table till you're full up to the muzzle.

My Country by Dorothea MacKellar (1911)

I love a sunburnt country,
A land of sweeping plains,
Of ragged mountain ranges,
Of droughts and flooding rains.
I love her far horizons,
I love her jewel-sea,
Her beauty and her terror,
This wide brown land for me.

The Man from Snowy River by Banjo Paterson (1890)

There was movement at the station, for the word had passed around
That the colt from old Regret had got away,
And had joined the wild bush horses, he was worth a thousand pound,
So all the cracks had gathered to the fray.
All the tried and noted riders from the stations near and far
Had mustered at the homestead overnight,
For the bushmen love hard riding where the wild bush horses are,
And the stock-horse snuffs the battle with delight.
And one was there, a stripling on a small and weedy beast,
He was something like a racehorse undersized,
With a touch of Timor pony, three parts thoroughbred at least,
And such as are by mountain horsemen prized.
He was hard and tough and wiry, just the sort that won't say die
There was courage in his quick impatient tread;
And he bore the badge of gameness in his bright and fiery eye,
And the proud and lofty carriage of his head.
And he ran them single-handed till their sides were white with foam.
He followed like a bloodhound on their track,
Till they halted cowed and beaten, then he turned their heads for home,
And alone and unassisted brought them back.
But his hardy mountain pony he could scarcely raise a trot,
He was blood from hip to shoulder from the spur;
But his pluck was still undaunted, and his courage fiery hot,
For never yet was mountain horse a cur.

The Overlander by unknown author (1880s)

There's a trade you all know well
And it's bringing cattle over,
On every track to the gulf and back
Men know the Queensland drover
So pass the billy round boys,
Don't let the pint pot stand there
For tonight we'll drink the health
Of every Overlander.

Nine miles from Gundagai by unknown author (1880s)

Some blokes I know has all the luck
No matter how they fall
But there was I, Lord love a duck,
No flamin' luck at all.
I couldn't make a pot of tea
Nor keep me trousers dry
And the dog shat in the tucker-box,
Nine miles from Gundagai.
I could forgive the blinkin' tea,
I could forgive the rain;
I could forgive the dark and cold,
And go through it again.
I could forgive me rotten luck,
But hang me till I die,
I won't forgive that bloody dog,
Nine miles from Gundagai.

Clancy of the Overflow by Banjo Paterson (1889)
(The narrator, working as a clerk in the city, remembers an old friend who
has gone droving in Queensland.)

And the bush hath friends to meet him, and their kindly voices greet him
In the murmur of the breezes and the river on its bars,
And he sees the vision splendid of the sunlit plains extended,
And at night the wond'rous glory of the everlasting stars.
I am sitting in my dingy little office, where a stingy
Ray of sunlight struggles feebly down between the houses tall,
And the foetid air and gritty of the dusty, dirty city
Through the open window floating, spreads its foulness over all.
And the hurrying people daunt me, and their pallid faces haunt me
As they shoulder one another in their rush and nervous haste,
With their eager eyes and greedy, and their stunted forms and weedy,
For townsfolk have no time to grow, they have no time to waste.
And I somehow rather fancy that I'd like to change with Clancy,
Like to take a turn at droving where the seasons come and go,
While he faced the round eternal of the cash-book and the journal —
But I doubt he'd suit the office, Clancy, of The Overflow.

Said Hanrahan by John O'Brien (1921)

'We'll all be rooned,' said Hanrahan,
In accents most forlorn,
Outside the church, ere Mass began,
One frosty Sunday morn.
The crops are done; ye'll have your work
To save one bag of grain;
From here way out to Back-o'-Bourke
They're singin' out for rain.
In God's good time down came the rain;
And all the afternoon
On iron roof and window-pane
It drummed a homely tune.
And every creek a banker ran,
And dams filled overtop;
'We'll all be rooned,' said Hanrahan,
'If this rain doesn't stop.'
And stop it did, in God's good time;
And spring came in to fold
A mantle o'er the hills sublime
Of green and pink and gold.
There'll be bush-fires for sure, me man,
There will, without a doubt;
'We'll all be rooned,' said Hanrahan,
'Before the year is out.'

West by North Again by Harry 'Breaker' Morant (1895)

We'll light our camp-fires where we may, and yarn beside their blaze;
The jingling hobble-chains shall make a music through the days.
And while the tucker-bags are right, and we've a stick of weed,
A swagman shall be welcome to a pipe-full and a feed.

So, fill your pipe! and, ere we mount, we'll drink another nip:
Here's how that West by North again may prove a lucky trip;
Then back again: I trust you'll find your best girl's merry face,
Or, if she jilts you, may you get a better in her place.

Best-loved brands

The most purchased products in Australian supermarkets are:

1 **Coca-Cola** soft drink
2 **Longbeach** cigarettes
3 **Pura** milk
4 **Tip Top** bread
5 **Huggies** disposable nappies
6 **Cadbury** chocolates
7 **Pedigree Pal** dog food
8 **Nescafé Blend 43** instant coffee
9 **Yoplait** yoghurt
10 **Sorbent** toilet paper
11 **Peters** ice-cream
12 **McCain** frozen vegetables
13 **Whiskas** cat food
14 **Colgate** toothpaste
15 **Kraft** cheese
16 **Smith's Crisps** snack food
17 **John West** canned fish
18 **Berri** fruit juice
19 **Gillette** razors
20 **Kleenex** tissues
21 **Pantene** shampoo
22 **Arnott's** biscuits
23 **Uncle Toby's** muesli bars
24 **Libra** tampons
25 **Flora** margarine
26 **Milo** milk modifier
27 **Old El Paso** Mexican foods
28 **San Remo** pasta*
29 **Kelloggs Nutri-Grain** cereal
30 **Heinz** baked beans and spaghetti
31 **Goulburn Valley** canned fruit
32 **Omo** laundry detergent
33 **Vegemite**
34 **Cottee's** cordials
35 **Leggo's** tomato products
36 **Heinz** baby foods
37 **Campbell's** soup
38 **McCain** frozen pizza
39 **Ingham's** frozen chicken*
40 **Glad** plastic wrap
41 **Rexona** deodorant

*Made by an Australian-owned company

Source: AC Nielsen

A day in the life

The list of the most popular supermarket products on the previous page enables us to visualise the typical consumption pattern for a typical suburban family. If you don't recognise yourself in this, you're simply un-Australian.

Morning: In the bathroom the family wipes with Sorbent, shampoos with Pantene and deodorises with Rexona. Dad shaves with Gillette, teenage daughter uses Libra tampons and baby is wrapped in Huggies disposables.

In the kitchen mum and dad drink Nescafé Blend 43 and pour Pura milk over Kellogg's Nutri-Grain, while daughter drinks Berri orange juice and spreads Vegemite on Arnott's Shapes. They feed Pedigree Pal to the dog and Whiskas to the cat. Around 10 a.m. mum puts on a wash with Omo and sips a cup of Lipton's tea. Dad chews Wrigley's Extra gum.

Afternoon: For lunch mum reheats some leftover spaghetti bolognese she made yesterday with Leggo's tomato sauce and San Remo pasta. She grates Kraft cheese over it. Daughter eats Yoplait yoghurt and an Uncle Toby's muesli bar. Dad eats sandwiches made from Tip Top white bread and John West canned tuna, and buys a takeaway cappuccino. Youngest family member eats Heinz baby food. After school, daughter snacks on Smith's Crisps and Coca-Cola.

Evening: For dinner the family eats Campbell's soup followed by a roasted Ingham's chicken with McCain vegetables. Mum and dad drink a glass of Queen Adelaide chardonnay. Dessert is Goulburn Valley canned fruit with Peters ice-cream. Then they cover the leftovers with Glad Wrap, brush their teeth with Colgate and switch on 'Home and Away'.

Our most interesting restaurants (2007)

1 **Tetsuya's**, Sydney: Japanese/French
2 **The Flower Drum**, Melbourne: Chinese
3 **Rockpool**, Sydney: Asian seafood
4 **Restaurant II**, Brisbane: French/Asian
5 **Taxi**, Melbourne: Japanese/European
6 **The Grange**, Adelaide: Asian
7 **Stefano's**, Mildura (Vic.): Italian
8 **Ottoman Cuisine**, Canberra: Turkish
9 **Buon Ricordo**, Sydney: Italian
10 **Lucio's**, Sydney: Italian
11 **Star Anise**, Perth: Asian
12 **Ezard at Adelphi**, Melbourne: Asian
13 **Marque**, Sydney: French
14 **Guillaume at Bennelong**, Sydney: French
15 **Vue de Monde**, Melbourne: French
16 **Sails**, Noosa (Qld): Italian/Asian
17 **The Bridgewater Mill**, Adelaide Hills: Asian/French
18 **Est.**, Sydney: French
19 **Courgette**, Canberra: French
20 **Fellini**, Surfers Paradise: Italian

Our media moments

In 2005 Britain's *Uncut* magazine published a list, chosen by an expert panel, of '100 mass media moments that changed the world'. Australians were as influenced as Britons and Americans by the events on the list, which was topped by Bob Dylan's 'Like a Rolling Stone' and Elvis Presley's 'Heartbreak Hotel'. It also included the films *A Clockwork Orange*, *Taxi Driver* and *The Godfather* as well as the television series' 'The Simpsons' and Patrick McGoohan's 'The Prisoner'. The Who's song 'My Generation' and 'Purple Haze' by Jimi Hendrix were in the top 20, as was Jack Kerouac's 1950's beatnik book *On the Road*.

But Australians also had a few landmarks in their own culture — moments that went beyond mere entertainment to achieve social symbolism or historical significance. Here's a first attempt at 100 media moments that changed Australia in the past 50 years.

1 **Graham Kennedy's** tonight shows (TV, 1957–91)

2 **Men At Work's** 'Down Under' (song, 1982)

3 **Germaine Greer's** *The Female Eunuch* (book, 1971)

4 **Barry Humphries** creates Edna Everage (recording, 1957)

5 **Peter Allen's** 'I Still Call Australia Home' (song, 1981)

6 **Number 96** shows the first bare breasts, the first gay kiss and the first terrorist bomb as a ratings booster (TV, 1972–75)

7 **Crocodile Dundee** (film, 1986)

8 **Midnight Oil's** 'Beds are Burning' (song, 1987)

9 **Homicide** tops the ratings (TV, 1966)

10 **Mad Max** (film, 1979)

11 **Bandstand** (TV, 1958–72)

12 **Wogs Out of Work** (stage, 1987)

13 **Barry Jones** wins *Pick-a-Box* (TV, 1960–71)

14 **AC/DC** make a video clip of 'It's a Long Way to the Top' (TV, 1977)

15 **Hugh Mackay's** *Reinventing Australia* (book, 1991)

16 **The Grim Reaper** commercials, warning about AIDS (advertising from 1987)

17 **Kath and Kim** (TV, 2001–)

18 **Picnic at Hanging Rock** (film, 1975)

19 **Oz** editors beat obscenity charges (magazines, 1964)

20 **Neighbours** (TV, 1986–)

21 **Yothu Yindi's** 'Treaty' (song, 1991)

22 **Normie Rowe** and **Ron Casey** fight over republicanism on the *Midday* show (TV, 1991)

23 **The Adventures of Priscilla, Queen of the Desert** (film, 1994)

24 **SeaChange** (TV, 1998–2000)

25 **John Farnham's** 'You're the Voice' (song, 1986)

26 **Sydney Olympics** opening ceremony (TV, 2000)

27 **Cleo** launches (magazine, 1972)

28 **Frontline** satirises *A Current Affair* (TV, 1994–97)

29 **Slim Dusty's** 'Pub With No Beer' (song, 1958)

30 **Kerry Packer** launches 'World Series Cricket' (TV, 1978)

31 The first **Top 40** chart published — by Sydney Radio 2UE (music, 1958)

32 **Bob Hawke** admits infidelity and cries, on Clive Robertson's 'Newsworld' (TV, 1989)

33 **Mambo** starts making loud shirts (fashion, 1985)

34 **The Mavis Bramston Show** (TV, 1964–68)

35 **SBS** starts multicultural programming (TV, 1980)

36 **Daddy Cool's** 'Eagle Rock' (music, 1971)

37 **The Block** features gay renovators (TV, 2003)

38 **Austen Tayshus'** *Australiana* (stage, 1983)

39 **McDonald's** introduces the McOz (food, 1999)

40 **Mother and Son** (TV, 1984–94)

41 **Triple J** rock radio goes national (music, 1995)

42 John O'Grady's book (1957) and the film (1966) of **They're A Weird Mob**

43 **60 Minutes** reporter Richard Carleton drops dead at the Beaconsfield mine rescue site (TV, 2006)

44 **Woman's Day** publishes paparazzi shots of a topless Duchess of York having her toes sucked (magazine, 1992)

45 **Alvin Purple** (film, 1973)

46 Robin Boyd's **The Australian Ugliness** (book, 1960)

47 **The Easybeats'** 'Friday on my Mind' (song, 1966)

48 **The Aunty Jack Show** changes from black and white to colour mid-episode (TV, 1975)

49 **Cold Chisel's** 'Khe Sanh' (song, 1978)

50 **Guy Sebastian** wins 'Australian Idol' (TV, 2003)

51 **Big Brother** contestant Merlin protests detention of boat people (TV, 2004)

52 **Barry Humphries** does Sir Les Patterson, Minister for The Yarts (stage, 1974–)

53 The governor-general, **Sir John Kerr**, is tired and emotional at the Melbourne Cup (TV, 1977)

54 **The Norman Gunston Show** (TV, 1973–76, 1993)

55 **Countdown**, and the rise of Molly Meldrum (TV, 1974–86)

56 English model **Jean Shrimpton** shocks Melbourne matrons by wearing a mini dress to the races (fashion, 1965)

57 PM **Bob Hawke** declares any boss 'a bum' if he penalises a worker for turning up late after celebrating Australia's win in the America's Cup (TV, 1983)

58 Designer **Ken Done** puts Australia's ocean colours on shirts, bags, hats, cards, etc (fashion, 1980–)

59 The **Moonlight State** episode of 'Four Corners' exposes police and political corruption in Queensland (TV, 1987)

60 Police arrest participants in the first **Sydney Mardi Gras** parade (1978) and become participants in the twenty-fifth Gay and Lesbian Mardi Gras parade (2003)

61 **Kylie Minogue** introduces her buttocks in the music video of 'Spinning Around' (TV, 2000)

62 **Gallipoli** (film, 1981)

63 **Talkback radio** starts replacing Top 40 radio (1967)

64 **Cathy Freeman's** 400 metres win at the Sydney Olympics (TV, 2000)

65 **Giant rubber kangaroos** on bicycles introduce (and embarrass) Australia at the end of the Atlanta Olympics (TV, 1996)

66 **Rolf Harris'** 'Tie Me Kangaroo Down, Sport' (song, 1960)

67 John Doyle and Greig Pickhaver do **Roy Slaven** and **H.G. Nelson** (radio and TV from 1986)

68 **Johnny O'Keefe** is the first successful Aussie rocker (song, TV, 1956–78)

69 The ABC's **This Day Tonight** starts aggressive questioning of politicians (TV, 1967)

70 **Russell Morris's** 'The Real Thing' (song, 1969)

71 **Charlie Cousins** falls off the wheat silo in 'Bellbird' (TV, 1967)

72 **Joe Dolce's** 'Shaddup You Face' (song, 1981)

73 **Steve Irwin** holds his baby while feeding a crocodile (TV, 2004)

74 **Pauline Hanson** moves from politician to celebrity in 'Dancing with the Stars' (TV, 2004)

75 **The Castle** (film, 1997)

76 **Eric Bogle's** 'And the Band Played Waltzing Matilda' (song, 1972)

77 **Mike Willesee** is tired and emotional hosting 'A Current Affair' on Channel 9, and the following week his rival on Channel 7 introduces himself by saying, 'I'm Derryn Hinch and I'm sober' (TV, 1989)

78 **Kerry Packer** pulls off Doug Mulray's 'Naughtiest Home Videos' halfway through the first episode (TV, 1997)

79 **Gough Whitlam** supports the National Gallery's purchase of Jackson Pollock's Blue Poles (art, 1974)

80 **Redgum** sings John Schumann's Vietnam War anthem 'Only Nineteen' (song, 1984)

81 **Ken Shorter** feels up Rowena Wallace in 'You Can't See Round Corners' (TV, 1967)

82 **John Williamson's** environmental song 'Rip Rip Woodchip' features in the NSW rugby league grand final entertainment (TV, 1999)

83 **'Life, Be In It'** commercials, with Norm (advertising, 1978–mid 1980s)

84 **Mary-Anne Fahey** does Kylie Mole on 'The Comedy Company' (TV, 1988)

85 The first **Lotto** draw (TV, 1983)

86 **Skyhooks'** album *Living in the 70's* (music, 1974)

87 **Muriel's Wedding** (film, 1994)

88 **Paul Hogan** promotes Australia with 'I'll slip an extra shrimp on the barbie' ads (TV, 1987–)

89 **Anne Summers's** *Damned Whores and God's Police* (book, 1973)

90 The ABC launches late night music video show **Rage** (TV, 1987)

91 The Australian classic **Newsfront** is released on DVD, and in the extras writer Bob Ellis calls himself 'stupid, stupid, stupid' (film, 2001)

92 Channel 10 forced to introduce new **censorship rules** after contestant Michael exposes his penis in 'Big Brother Uncut' (TV, 2005)

93 Channel 10 expels contestants Ash and John from the **Big Brother** house for turkey slapping contestant Camilla (TV, 2006)

94 **Molly Jones's** death in 'A Country Practice' is delayed for two weeks to ensure it happens in a ratings period (TV, 1984)

95 A historical mini-series, **Against the Wind**, tops the ratings (TV, 1988)

96 Children's group **Hi-5** sell more videos and albums than children's group The Wiggles (music, TV, 2003)

97 **Charlene** (Kylie Minogue) **marries Scott** (Jason Donovan) in 'Neighbours' (TV, 1987)

98 The end of Australia's longest running sitcom **Hey Dad** (TV, 1994)

99 **Border Security**, a documentary about the Customs service, becomes Australia's most watched series (TV, 2005)

100 **John Paul Young's** 'Love is in the Air' (song, 1982)

6

OUR KIND OF PEOPLE

Stirrers

Geoffrey Blainey

A Melbourne historian and author of a standard text about Australia, *The Tyranny of Distance*, Blainey suggested in the 1980s that multiculturalism was turning Australia into 'a cluster of tribes', that immigration from Asia should be slowed down, and that relations between Aborigines and white settlers had not been as negative as portrayed by 'the black armband view of history'.

Bob Brown

A Green politician elected to the Senate in 1996 and 2001 by Tasmanians, Brown has been Australia's most consistent opposition leader since the election of John Howard, criticising Australia's detention of asylum seekers, the sending of troops to Iraq, the weakening of industrial relations laws, and the neglect of Aboriginal health.

Helen Caldicott

Adelaide-trained doctor and campaigner against nuclear weapons and nuclear power, Caldicott is president of the Washington-based Nuclear Power Research Institute.

Paul Davies

England-born professor of natural philosophy at Macquarie University in Sydney, Davies' efforts to reconcile science and faith have been translated around the globe, notably in his books *The Mind of God, God and the New Physics, The Edge of Infinity, The Cosmic Blueprint, Are We Alone?* and *How to Build a Time Machine*.

Tim Flannery

A Melbourne-born environmentalist and director of the South Australian Museum, Flannery argues, in *The Future Eaters*, that Australia needs to cut its population to below 18 million, and suggests, in *The Weather Makers*, that nuclear power would be less damaging than other energy sources.

Peter Garrett

Sydney-born Labor MP for Kingsford-Smith electorate in New South Wales and former singer with Midnight Oil, Garrett once wrote songs attacking American militarism, supported Aboriginal land rights and an Australian republic, and stood as a Senate candidate for the Nuclear Disarmament Party. His fans wonder if he'll be as outspoken now that he's a mainstream politician.

Germaine Greer

Melbourne-born, England-resident author and teacher, Greer launched modern feminism with *The Female Eunuch* in 1970, and continues to provoke her compatriots with books and pronouncements on male beauty, menopause, Aboriginal reconciliation, and Australians being 'too relaxed to give a damn'.

Donald Horne

New South Wales-born activist for a republic and former chair of the cultural funding body The Australia Council, Horne's 1964 book, *The Lucky Country*, said 'Australia is a lucky country, run by second-rate people who share its luck'. He died in 2005.

Jack Mundey

Queensland-born former leader of the New South Wales branch of the Builders Labourers Federation, Mundey argued in the 1970s that workers had the right and duty to strike for environmental reasons as well as for financial reasons, and they should use 'green bans' to protect wilderness areas and heritage buildings.

Philip Nitschke

Adelaide-born doctor and activist for the right of terminally ill patients to end their own lives, Nitschke persuaded the Northern Territory parliament in 1997 to legalise voluntary euthanasia, but this was later overturned by the federal government.

John Pilger

Sydney-born, London-resident journalist and documentary maker, Pilger exposes the machinations of multinationals and the hypocrisy of governments. Some fans wish he could combine his investigative skills with Michael Moore's sense of humour, but some scandals just aren't funny.

Peter Singer

Melbourne-born professor of bioethics at the Centre for Human Values, Princeton University, and author of *Practical Ethics, Rethinking Life and Death, Animal Rights and Human Obligations* and *The President of Good and Evil*, Singer supports abortion, animal liberation and euthanasia.

Dick Smith

A Sydney-born businessman, Smith sold his retail chain, Dick Smith Electronics, in 1982 to devote himself to adventure and activism, making the first solo helicopter flight around the world and launching Dick Smith Foods in 1999 to promote Australian ownership of popular products.

Investigators

Graeme Clark

Sydney-born Professor of Otolaryngology at the University of Melbourne, Clark's invention of the bionic ear, or 'multi-channel cochlear implant', has helped 60 000 deaf adults to hear.

Derek Denton

Launceston-born founder of the Howard Florey Institute of Experimental Physiology and Medicine at the University of Melbourne, Denton discovered the link between salt and high blood pressure.

Peter Doherty

Brisbane-born Professor of Microbiology and Immunology at Melbourne University and Professor of Pediatrics at the University of Tennessee, Doherty won a Nobel Prize for Medicine in 1996 for 'discoveries concerning the specificity of the cell-mediated immune defence'.

(Australia's other Nobel-Prize winning scientists have been William Lawrence Bragg and his father, William Henry Bragg, for X-ray crystallography in 1915; Howard Florey for work on antibiotics in 1945; Frank Macfarlane Burnet for immunology in 1960; John Eccles for study of the nervous system in 1963; John Cornforth for study of enzyme catalysed reactions in 1973; and Barry Marshall and Robin Warren in 2005 for discovering the role of bacteria in ulcers.)

Ian Frazer

Edinburgh-born, Dr Frazer now heads the University of Queensland Centre for Immunology and Cancer Research at the Princess Alexandra Hospital, Brisbane. He was named Australian of the Year 2006 for developing a vaccine which prevents disease associated with the papilloma virus that causes most cervical cancers.

Basil Hetzel

London-born Professor of Medicine at The Queen Elizabeth Hospital, University of Adelaide, Foundation Professor of Social and Preventive Medicine at Monash University, and the First Chief of the CSIRO Division of Human Nutrition, Hetzel's work helped eradicate iodine deficiency in many countries.

Silviu Itescu

Melbourne-trained director of transplantation immunology at Columbia University Medical Centre in New York, Itescu showed that adult stem cells from bone marrow could be used to repair damaged hearts.

Barry Marshall

Kalgoorlie-born gastroenterologist at the University of Western Australia, Marshall defeated sceptics by swallowing a culture of the bacteria *Helicobacter pylori*, giving himself gastritis, then curing it with antibiotics, while investigating the cause of stomach ulcers with pathologist Robin Warren in the mid-1980s. This transformed the way most ulcers are tested and treated. In 2005, Marshall and Warren won the Nobel prize for medicine.

Robert May

Sydney-born president of the Royal Society in London, May studied theoretical physics at Sydney University and mathematical biology at Oxford then became chief scientific adviser to the British Government. He specialises in the dynamics of populations, communities and ecosystems, looking at the impact of AIDS, biodiversity and global warming.

William McBride

The allegations that Sydney-born gynaecologist McBride took ethical shortcuts in his later research do not diminish his discovery in the 1960s that the morning sickness drug thalidomide caused deformities in babies.

Donald Metcalf

New South Wales-born Professor Emeritus at the Walter and Eliza Hall Institute of Medical Research in Melbourne, Metcalf discovered 'colony stimulating factors' in blood cell formation, which revolutionised the treatment of cancer and earned him the title 'the father of hematopoietic cytokines'.

Gustav Nossal

Austrian-born adviser to the World Health Organisation on eradicating childhood diseases, Nossal, after thirty years of directing medical research at Melbourne's Walter and Eliza Hall Institute, now chairs the $A1.4 billion Bill and Melinda Gates Program for immunising children in poor nations.

Kennedy Shortridge

Queensland-born Emeritus Professor of Microbiology at the University of Hong Kong, Shortridge's research on the spread of respiratory viruses from poultry to humans is credited with averting an influenza pandemic in 1997.

Allan Snyder

US-born Professor of Science and the Mind at the Australian National University, Snyder's research on how light travels along optical fibres is central to modern telecommunications technology. He also founded the Centre for the Mind at the ANU to investigate the talents of autistic savants and the potential of the brain.

Fiona Stanley

Sydney-born chief executive of Perth's Australian Research Alliance for Children and Youth, Stanley's investigations into the causes and prevention of birth defects and neurological disorders led her to become a lobbyist on behalf of underprivileged children.

Communicators

Col Allan

NSW-born former editor of Rupert Murdoch's Sydney tabloid the *Daily Telegraph*, Allan became the editor in 2003 of Murdoch's main American tabloid *The New York Post*, and earns $US 600 000 a year.

Peter Carey

Melbourne-born novelist and former head of a Sydney advertising agency, Carey won the Miles Franklin Award for the novel *Bliss* in 1981, then Britain's Booker Prize in 1988 for *Oscar and Lucinda* and in 2001 for *The True History of the Kelly Gang*.

J.M. Coetzee

South African-born and Adelaide-resident novelist, John Maxwell Coetzee won the Booker Prize in 1983 for *Life and Times of Michael K* and again in 1999 for *Disgrace*, and then won the Nobel Prize for Literature in 2003 as an author 'who in innumerable guises portrays the surprising involvement of the outsider'.

Bryce Courtenay

South African-born ex-advertising executive, Courtenay is our most successful author, totalling three million sales for his novels, including *The Power of One*, *The Potato Factory*, *Tommo and Hawk*, *Jessica* and *Solomon's Song*.

Helen Garner

Melbourne-born writer Garner has moved from novels such as *Monkey Grip* to social analyses such as *The First Stone* (about sexual harassment) and *Joe Cinque's Consolation* (about drug addiction and murder).

Robert Hughes

Sydney-born art critic for *Time* magazine, Hughes became one of America's most influential social commentators through such books as *Culture of Complaint*, *American Visions*, *Nothing if Not Critical* and *The Shock of the New*.

Clive James

Sydney-born writer, poet, critic and comedian, James is one of Britain's most influential media commentators, best known here for his hilarious autobiography *Unreliable Memoirs*.

Thomas Keneally

Sydney-born novelist and activist for a republic, Keneally won Britain's Booker Prize for *Schindler's Ark* (adapted by Steven Spielberg as the film *Schindler's List*) and analysed Australia's hang-ups with *Bring Larks and Heroes, The Chant of Jimmy Blacksmith* and *The Cut Rate Kingdom*.

Jill Ker Conway

New South Wales-born writer Conway wrote an autobiographical series starting with *The Road from Coorain*, ran Smith College, America's largest university for women, and was chairman of Lend Lease for two difficult years.

Rupert Murdoch

Melbourne-born chief executive of US-based News Corporation, Murdoch controls media on most continents through such outlets as Fox, Sky, *The Times* and *The Australian*, but failed to dissuade his son Lachlan from leaving his job with News Corp in New York and returning to Sydney. Now Murdoch's heir-apparent seems to be his younger son James.

Les Murray

Country New South Wales-born poet, Murray's collections include *The Vernacular Republic, Lunch and Counter Lunch* and *Subhuman Redneck Poems*, which won the T.S. Eliot literary prize in 1996.

David Nunan

Broken Hill-born professor of applied linguistics at the University of Hong Kong, Nunan's teachings have spread the English language throughout Asia. Students in Japan, South Korea and China buy more than a million copies of his textbooks every year.

Kerry Packer

Sydney-born chairman of Consolidated Press Holdings, Packer built an empire that included the Channel 9 network and Australia's top-selling magazines, such as *Women's Weekly* and *Woman's Day*, as well as casinos on three continents. Packer died in December 2005, leaving his son James, who is keen to move the company into new media.

Wilga Rivers

A Melbourne-born linguist and professor emerita of romance languages and literature at Harvard University, Rivers has been awarded the Legion d'Honneur by the French Government.

Dorothy Rowe

Newcastle-born psychologist Rowe was voted one of the six wisest people in Britain in the 1990s for her books and TV appearances on conquering fear and depression.

Robert Thomson

Victoria-born journalist Thomson trained at the *Sydney Morning Herald* and became editor of *The Times* of London in 2004.

David Williamson

A Melbourne-born engineer by training, Williamson is our most successful playwright and screenwriter, with hits such as *The Removalists, Don's Party, The Club, Gallipoli, Emerald City* and *Phar Lap*.

Tim Winton

Perth-born novelist Winton won the Miles Franklin Award for *The Shallows* in 1984, *Cloudstreet* in 1992 and *Dirt Music* in 2002.

Helpers

David Bussau

New Zealand-born, Sydney-based founder of Opportunity International, Bussau tackles poverty by arranging loans to small businesses in developing countries.

Simon Chesterman

Melbourne-born executive director of the Institute for International Law and Justice at New York University, Chesterman is the author of *Just War or Just Peace? Humanitarian Intervention and International Law*. He advises the UN on helping countries make the transition from dictatorship to democracy.

John Fawcett

Perth-born Bali-based international projects director for the John Fawcett Foundation, Fawcett's clinics treat thousands of Indonesian children with diseases of the eyes, palate and chest.

Rowan Gillies

Sydney-born president of *Medecins Sans Frontieres* (Doctors Without Borders), Gillies travels to crisis spots around the world, organising medical aid.

Catherine Hamlin

Sydney-born director of Addis Ababa Fistula Hospital in Ethiopia, Hamlin has spent the past 44 years performing and teaching surgery for women injured while giving birth.

Fred Hollows

A New Zealand-born opthalmologist who spent 30 years trying to prevent blindness caused by trachoma among Aboriginal people. He died in 1993, but his foundation continues to build clinics and lens factories throughout Africa and Asia.

Ian Kiernan

Sydney-born businessman, yachtsman and environmentalist Kiernan was alarmed by the extent of ocean pollution in the 1990s and organised the Clean Up Australia movement, which has now grown into the Clean Up The World movement with 40 million volunteers in 120 countries.

Mahboba Rawi

Kabul-born, Sydney-based founder of the aid agency Mahboba's Promise, Rawi escaped Afghanistan as a refugee and now returns to build orphanages, schools and hospitals for women and children.

Entertainers

Gillian Armstrong

Melbourne-born director Armstrong won an Australian Film Institute (AFI) award for her film of *My Brilliant Career* but is best known in America for *Little Women* and *Charlotte Gray*.

Bruce Beresford

Sydney-born director Beresford won AFI awards for his films *The Fringe Dwellers*, *Breaker Morant* and *Don's Party*, and was Oscar-nominated for *Tender Mercies*. He is best known for *Driving Miss Daisy*.

Cate Blanchett

Melbourne-born actress Blanchett won an Oscar for her role in *The Aviator*, a BAFTA and a Golden Globe for *Elizabeth*, an AFI for *Thank God He Met Lizzie*, and is much admired for her Galadriel in *The Lord of the Rings* trilogy.

Bryan Brown

Sydney-born actor/producer Brown won AFI awards for his roles in *Breaker Morant* and *Two Hands* and perfected the blunt but decent Aussie persona in *Cocktail*, *Gorillas in the Mist*, *Tai Pan* and *A Town Like Alice*.

Jane Campion

New Zealand-born and Sydney-trained director Campion won an AFI for her film *Sweetie* and an Oscar for *The Piano*. She also made *Portrait of a Lady*, *In The Cut* and *Angel at My Table*.

Nick Cave

Melbourne-born, London-based singer and composer Cave, a former heroin addict, is better known for albums than singles, and his tortured punk ballads include 'From Her To Eternity', 'Tupelo', 'Sad Waters', 'Into My Arms' and 'The Weeping Song'. In 2005 he wrote an Australian 'Western' movie, *The Proposition*.

Toni Collette

Sydney-born actress Collete was Oscar-nominated for her role in *The Sixth Sense*, and won AFI awards for *Muriel's Wedding*, *Lillian's Story*, *The Boys* and *Japanese Story*. In 2006, she attempted a singing career.

Russell Crowe

New Zealand-born, Sydney-trained actor Crowe is best known for his bad temper and winning an Oscar for *Gladiator*, a BAFTA for *A Beautiful Mind*, and AFIs for *Romper Stomper* and *Proof*.

Judy Davis

Perth-born actress Davis was Oscar-nominated for *Husbands and Wives* and *A Passage to India*, and won a BAFTA for *My Brilliant Career*, AFIs for *Winter of Our Dreams*, *High Tide* and *Children of the Revolution*, and an Emmy for *Life With Judy Garland*.

Mel Gibson

New York-born, Sydney-trained actor/director/producer Gibson is best known here for the *Mad Max* trilogy and internationally for making (with his Icon Films partner Bruce Davey) *The Passion of the Christ*. He won AFIs for *Tim* and *Gallipoli*, and an Oscar for directing *Braveheart*, and court-ordered alcoholism treatment for making anti-semetic remarks to a traffic cop in 2006.

Delta Goodrem

Sydney-born singer, pianist and composer Goodrem had hits with the singles 'Born to Try' and 'Lost Without You' and her album *Innocent Eyes* after starring in the teen soap 'Neighbours'.

Rachel Griffiths

Melbourne-born actress Griffiths was Oscar-nominated for her role as Hilary in *Hilary and Jackie*, and won an AFI for *Muriel's Wedding* and a Golden Globe for the TV series 'Six Feet Under'.

Reg Grundy

Sydney-born television game show host and producer Grundy created 'Sale of the Century', 'The Restless Years', 'Prisoner' and 'Neighbours' here, then built an international empire of more than 200 dramas and game shows.

Rolf Harris

Perth-born singer and comedian Harris's wobble board carried Australia's image to London, to the tune of 'Tie Me Kangaroo Down, Sport', long before Kylie's buttocks and Elle's breasts.

Jennifer Hawkins

Newcastle-born model who won the Miss Universe contest in 2004, Hawkins created a television career by appearances in 'The Great Outdoors', 'Dancing with the Stars' and Myer commercials. She was the best looking person on TV in 2006.

Paul Hogan

Lightning Ridge-born actor Hogan made his name in the 1970s with TV sketch comedy and then created our most successful international movie, *Crocodile Dundee*. He also 'put another shrimp on the barbie' in tourism commercials. In 2006 he was investigated by the Tax Office.

Barry Humphries

Melbourne-born comedian Humphries has made Dame Edna Everage the toast of London and New York stage and television, while his politician Sir Les Patterson keeps coming home to haunt us.

Natalie Imbruglia

Sydney-born singer and composer Imbruglia starred in the teen soap 'Neighbours' before moving to London and recording the number-one single 'Torn'. She is married to the singer-composer Daniel Johns (ex silverchair).

Steve Irwin

Melbourne-born presenter of the TV documentary series 'Crocodile Hunter', Irwin became world notorious in 2004 for feeding a crocodile while holding his baby son. He was killed by a stingray in 2006.

Hugh Jackman

Sydney-born actor/singer Jackman won a Tony award for his Broadway portrayal of Peter Allen in *The Boy from Oz*, and then played amnesic lycanthropes in *Van Helsing* and the *X-Men* series of films.

Nicole Kidman

Hawaii-born, Sydney-trained actress Kidman is our highest paid performer, winning an Oscar for *The Hours*, a Golden Globe for *Moulin Rouge*, and an AFI for the TV miniseries 'Vietnam'.

Anthony LaPaglia

Adelaide-born actor LaPaglia is best known for playing New York cops and criminals. He won an AFI for *Lantana*, and a Golden Globe for the TV series 'Without a Trace'.

Heath Ledger

Perth-born actor Ledger is best known for his bad temper and roles in *Brokeback Mountain*, *Ned Kelly*, *The Patriot*, *Two Hands*, *A Knight's Tale*, *10 Things I Hate About You* and 'Home and Away'.

Baz Luhrman

New South Wales-born director Luhrman was Oscar-nominated for his film *Moulin Rouge*, and won an AFI for *Strictly Ballroom*, and a BAFTA for *Romeo+Juliet*.

Charles Mackerras

US-born, Sydney-trained oboist and conductor Mackerras has been chief conductor of opera companies throughout Europe and conducted the first concert for the opening of the Sydney Opera House in 1973.

Elle Macpherson

Sydney-born model, actress and entrepreneuse Macpherson was nicknamed 'The Body' after she became our first international supermodel. She also acted in *Sirens*, *The Edge*, *Batman and Robin*, and the TV series 'Friends'.

Jacqueline McKenzie

Sydney-born actress McKenzie won an AFI for *Angel Baby*, and is best known with an American accent in the TV series 'The 4400'.

Ray Martin

Sydney-born former presenter of 'A Current Affair' and 'Midday', Martin was once regarded as the most credible journalist/interviewer on commercial television. He has won several Logie awards and now narrates occasional features for Channel 9 programs, such as '60 Minutes'.

George Miller

Queensland-born director Miller won AFIs for *Flirting*, *The Year My Voice Broke* and *Mad Max 2* and was Oscar-nominated for *Babe* and *Lorenzo's Oil*. A different (Scottish-born) George Miller directed *The Man from Snowy River* and the TV series 'ANZACs' and 'All the Rivers Run'.

Kylie Minogue

Melbourne-born singer and dancer Minogue first starred in 'Neighbours' and then had a hit in 1988 with 'Locomotion'. She moved to London and made sexy music videos to promote 'Spinning Around' and 'Can't Get You Out of My Head', which attracted a gay male following. She returned to performing in 2006 after treatment for breast cancer.

Radha Mitchell

Melbourne-born actress Mitchell is best known for *Melinda and Melinda*, *Finding Neverland*, *Man on Fire*, *Pitch Black* and 'Neighbours'.

Simon Morley, Justin Morley and David Friend

Melbourne-born comedians Morley, Morley and Friend exported their 'genital origami' show *Puppetry of the Penis* to the world.

Sam Neill

Ireland-born, New Zealand-raised actor Neill is claimed by us because he won an AFI for *A Cry in the Dark* and played Australians in *My Brilliant Career*, 'Mary Bryant', 'Jessica', *The Dish*, *Sirens* and *Dead Calm*, and talked American almost as fluently as Australian actors in the two *Jurassic Park* films.

Phillip Noyce

Griffith-born director Noyce won AFIs for *Newsfront* and *Rabbit-Proof Fence* but is best known for the thrillers *Dead Calm*, *Patriot Games*, *Clear and Present Danger* and *Sliver*.

Frances O'Connor

England-born and Perth-raised actress O'Connor is best known here for *Kiss or Kill*, in Britain for *Madame Bovary* and *Mansfield Park* and in the US for *Bedazzled* and *AI: Artificial Intelligence*.

Miranda Otto

Brisbane-born actress Otto played Lindy Chamberlain in the TV miniseries 'Through My Eyes', and is best known in the US for the *Lord of the Rings* trilogy and *War of the Worlds*.

Guy Pearce

England-born and Geelong-raised actor Pearce began his career as a muscleman in 'Neighbours' and is now famously skinny. He starred in *The Adventures of Priscilla, Queen of the Desert*, *LA Confidential*, *Memento*, *The Time Machine* and *Two Brothers*.

Richard Roxburgh

Albury-born actor Roxburgh won an AFI for *Doing Time For Patsy Cline* and then got typecast as a villain in *Moulin Rouge*, *Mission Impossible 2*, *Van Helsing* and *The League of Extraordinary Gentlemen*.

Geoffrey Rush

Toowoomba-born actor Rush won an Oscar for *Shine*, a BAFTA for *Elizabeth*, a Golden Globe for *The Life and Death of Peter Sellers*, and acclaim from children for *Pirates of the Caribbean*.

Fred Schepisi

Melbourne-born director Schepisi won AFIs for *A Cry in the Dark* and *The Devil's Playground*, and is best known for *Roxanne*, *The Russia House* and *Last Orders*.

John Seale

Queensland-born cinematographer Seale won an AFI for *Careful, He Might Hear You* and an Oscar for *The English Patient*, and was Oscar-nominated for *Witness*, *Rain Man* and *Cold Mountain*.

Dean Semler

South Australia-born cinematographer Semler won an Oscar for *Dances with Wolves* and AFIs for *Dead Calm* and *My First Wife*, and is best known for *City Slickers*, *Bruce Almighty* and *The Longest Yard*.

Barry Tuckwell

Melbourne-born classical trumpeter Tuckwell was the most recorded horn player in the world, with 45 albums and three Grammy nominations, before he retired in the 1990s.

Naomi Watts

England-born, Sydney raised actress who started in the soap 'Home and Away' in 1991 and got noticed by Hollywood in 2001 after her role in *Mulholland Drive*. She was nominated for an Oscar and a BAFTA for *21 Grams*, and starred in *The Ring* and *King Kong*.

Hugo Weaving

Nigeria-born, Sydney-trained actor Weaving won AFIs for *Proof* and *The Interview*, found fame in *The Adventures of Priscilla, Queen of the Desert* and became our biggest box-office name with the *Lord of the Rings* and *Matrix* trilogies.

Peter Weir

Sydney-born director Weir won an AFI for *Gallipoli*, BAFTAs for *Dead Poets Society*, *The Truman Show* and *Master and Commander*, and was Oscar-nominated for *Green Card* and *Witness*, but he is best remembered here for restarting our film industry in 1975 with *Picnic at Hanging Rock*.

Jana Wendt

Melbourne-born presenter and interviewer, Wendt's intense manner and dramatic cheekbones made her a TV drawcard since the early 1980s for '60 Minutes', 'A Current Affair', and ABC and SBS news programs. In 2006 Channel 9 paid her $2 million to go quietly from her hosting job on 'Sunday'.

David Wenham

Sydney-born actor Wenham won an AFI for *Gettin' Square* and a Logie for 'SeaChange', and hit world eyes in the *Lord of the Rings* and *Van Helsing*.

Politicians

Joh Bjelke-Petersen

Premier of Queensland from 1968 to 1987, Bjelke-Petersen's National–Country Party held power due to a gerrymander: the size of electorates meant country members needed fewer voters than city members to win a seat. He presided over police corruption and intensive development, favouring roads through rainforests and oil drilling on the Great Barrier Reef.

Peter Costello

Liberal treasurer since 1996, Costello is thought to be a closet republican and sympathiser with Aborigines; expected to become prime minister if John Howard ever retires.

Don Dunstan

Labor premier of South Australia from 1970 to 1979, Dunstan continued South Australia's tradition of social reform when he legalised abortion and homosexuality, and introduced consumer protection laws.

Malcom Fraser

Liberal prime minister from 1975 to 1983, Fraser is best known for pro-environment views and for appearing without pants in the lobby of a hotel in Memphis, Tennessee, one morning in 1986, after apparently being drugged and robbed.

Bob Hawke

Labor prime minister from 1983 to 1991, Hawke was more famous for charisma, crying on television, beer drinking and womanising than for political decisions.

Pauline Hanson

Founder of the One Nation Party and independent Queensland MP from 1996 to 1999, Hansen articulated the fears of some impoverished Australians about immigrants taking their jobs and Aborigines receiving special treatment.

John Howard

Howard became Liberal prime minister in 1996, and is best known for introducing a 10 per cent Goods and Services Tax, committing Australian troops to join America in Iraq, and getting tough on unions and would be immigrants.

Paul Keating

Labor treasurer from 1983 and prime minister from 1991 to 1996, Keating introduced land rights for Aboriginal people and economic reforms that allowed business and banks to flourish, but alienated voters with his apparent arrogance.

Robert Menzies

Founder of the Liberal Party and prime minister from 1949 to 1965, Menzies was a father figure in a serious suit and a symbol of stability for a nation undergoing social change.

Henry Parkes

Premier of New South Wales in the 1870s and 1880s, Parkes was a campaigner for free public education and the federation of the colonies into a single nation, but did not live to see his plan fulfilled.

Gough Whitlam

Labor prime minister from 1972 to 1975, Whitlam was elected with a program of radical reform after 23 years of conservative government. He moved too fast and was dismissed by the governor-general, John Kerr, after the opposition, under Malcolm Fraser, blocked the budget.

Artists

John Coburn

An abstract painter born in 1925, Coburn designed the Sun and Moon tapestry curtains of the Sydney Opera House.

Patrick Cook

Australia's most savage political and sociological cartoonist, Cook currently draws for *The Bulletin*.

Grace Cossington Smith

Van Gogh-influenced Cossington Smith established the Modern Movement in Sydney. She died in 1984.

Denton Corker Marshall (DCM)

An architecture and design firm, DCM has, since 1972, transformed the look of the southern capital via the Melbourne Museum, the Exhibition Centre and a 'gateway' of coloured rods sticking up at an angle over the airport freeway. They also designed Brisbane Square, the Museum of Sydney and the Macquarie and Phillip Towers in Sydney. The partners' first names are John, Bill and Barrie.

Philip Cox

An adventurous architect who specialises in big public structures, Cox is behind such landmarks as the Sydney Football Stadium, Sydney's Darling Harbour Exhibition Centre and Yulara Resort near Uluru.

Ken Done

Done's colourful designs for million-selling tourist souvenirs have overshadowed his more serious paintings.

Max Dupain

His photos of sunbathers and city life became part of the visual definition of Australia. He died in 1992.

Walter Burley Griffin

An American disciple of Frank Lloyd Wright, Griffin designed Canberra, the New South Wales town of Griffith, the Melbourne suburbs of Heidelberg and Eaglemont, and the Sydney suburb of Castlecrag. He died in 1937.

Pro Hart

Born and based in Broken Hill, Hart painted the colours and creatures of the Australian desert and did the occasional TV commercial for carpet cleaners. He died in 2006.

Rover Thomas Joolama

Joolama began using earth pigment on board in the Kimberley region of Western Australia. He died in 1996, but his works now fetch up to $1 million.

Emily Kame Kngwarreye

A ceremonial painter of rock and bark from Utopia, 200 kilometres east of Alice Springs, Kngwarreye began using modern materials to paint desert life after she turned 70. She died in 1996.

Colin Lanceley

Lanceley blends sculpture and painting into three-dimensional works.

Bill Leak

He draws vicious political caricatures for *The Australian* newspaper, and paints serious portraits for the Archibald Prize competition which, he says, he has lost more times than any living artist.

Michael Leunig

Leunig is a whimsical cartoonist, pop philosopher and creator of eccentric characters. He has produced books, TV animations, and illustrations for *The Age* and the *Sydney Morning Herald* newspapers.

Norman Lindsay

Best known for shocking polite society through painting, etching and sculpting naked ladies at his Blue Mountains home near Sydney, Lindsay lives on as the creator of *The Magic Pudding*. He died in 1969.

Frederick McCubbin and Tom Roberts

They set up an artists' colony outside Melbourne in the 1890s and were the first to capture the real colours of the Australian bush, founding the Heidelberg School of Australian impressionism which has influenced landscape painting to this day. McCubbin died in 1917, Roberts in 1931.

Glenn Murcutt

Murcutt's low-rise architectural projects, using materials such as corrugated iron to give an outback appearance, are designed to blend into the environment. In 1992, he won the Alvar Aalto Medal in Finland and in 2001 the international Pritzker Prize.

Sidney Nolan

He painted in series, showing how a place or a story changed over time, and is best known for his Ned Kelly series. He died in 1992.

John Olsen

A painter of outback landscapes, Olsen won the Sulman Prize in 1989 and the Archibald Prize in 2005 for a self-portrait (in an outback landscape).

Bruce Petty

Petty is the nation's most uncompromising, complex and perceptive political cartoonist, originally for *The Australian* and now for *The Age*.

Harry Seidler

An architect of Austrian background, Seidler pioneered the skyscraper in Sydney with Australia Square Tower, the Blues Point Tower, the Horizon Building and the MLC Centre. He died in 2006.

Martin Sharp

Emerging in the 1960s as our top pop artist, Sharp designed psychedelic posters and homages to comic characters such as Ginger Meggs and Boofhead.

Jeffrey Smart

Smart's paintings are detailed urban scenes approaching 'hyperrealism'.

Clifford Possum Tjapaltjarri

Tjapaltjarri's dot paintings, which tell elaborate dreaming stories, started the craze for Aboriginal art. He died in 2002.

Brett Whiteley

Best known for heroin addiction and big blue harbour scenes, Whiteley won the Archibald Prize in 1978. He died in 1992.

Cathy Wilcox

Drawing single-column gags for the *Sydney Morning Herald* and *The Age*, Wilcox is the nation's sharpest political cartoonist on a small scale.

Pioneers of a new Australia

Stephanie Alexander

After running Stephanie's, Melbourne's most interesting restaurant, for 21 years Alexander retired from daily cooking and set about writing the bible of ingredients available in Australia and techniques learned from the multitude of cultures that have joined our population. *The Cook's Companion*, first published in 1996 and revised in 2004, is 816 pages long and has sold half a million copies.

Geoffrey Atherden

Australia's most thoughtful and original TV comedy writer, Atherden began with scripts for 'The Aunty Jack Show' in the early 1970s and went on to win multiple awards for creating the sitcoms 'Mother and Son' and 'Grass Roots'.

Circus Oz

Replacing animal acts with rock music and slapstick with political satire, Circus Oz started in Melbourne in 1978 and by 2005 had performed in 26 countries, stimulating an international boom in 'physical theatre'. From the founding members only Tim Coldwell still performs with the troupe, but the newer acrobats and clowns share the original egalitarian philosophy.

John Clarke

Although born in New Zealand and still sounding like it, Clarke is Australia's 21st century court jester, interviewed regularly by Bryan Dawe on 'The 7.30 Report' in the guise of the most ridiculous politician of the day. His satirical TV series 'The Games' anticipated most of the hypocrisy that happened during the 2000 Olympics. He wrote a public apology to Aboriginal people which was delivered by John Howard (the actor from 'All Saints'). An excerpt:

> 'Our forebears, fighting to establish themselves in what they saw as a harsh environment, were creating a national economy. But the Aboriginal world was decimated. A pattern of disease and dispossession was established. Social and racial differences were allowed to become fault-lines. I speak for all Australians in expressing a profound sorrow to the Aboriginal people. I am sorry. We are sorry. Let the world know and

understand that it is with this sorrow that we as a nation will grow and seek a better, a fairer and a wiser future.'

Hector Crawford

Using the radio production house he founded in Melbourne in 1946, Crawford became the first independent maker of drama for Australian television, generating series such as 'Consider Your Verdict', 'Homicide', 'The Box', 'Cop Shop', 'Division 4', 'All the Rivers Run' and 'The Sullivans'. He died in 1991. His risky vision for Australian drama was first vindicated in 1966, when news came through that 'Homicide' was out-rating a popular US series called 'The Fugitive', and the TV critic Harry Robinson wrote:

'The importance, of course, is not that "Homicide" is doing well, but rather that Australians may at last be willing to consider their own people with their own ways worth watching. Till now, as any showman will tell you, Australians have preferred to watch anybody but their own kind, no matter what the quality. Perhaps we have grown up enough to give ourselves a fair go.'

Cheong Liew

Malaysian-born of Chinese parents, Cheong learned to cook in Greek and French restaurants in Adelaide and introduced the East meets West or 'fusion cuisine' craze to Australia in the 1980s. Still experimenting at The Grange restaurant in Adelaide, he says:

'To do fusion properly a chef should be fluent in five culinary languages. Fusion demonstrates what we have achieved as humans in terms of the marriage and harmony of ingredients as well as people and cultures — it's really about multiculturalism in our society.'

Serge Dansereau

A French-Canadian chef hired to build an international reputation for Sydney's Regent Hotel, Dansereau arrived in 1981 to find a dearth of diversity in our salads. Bored by iceberg lettuce, he experimented with imported seeds and used the hotel's buying power to encourage growers to plant such unfamiliar leaves as rocket, chervil, endive, radicchio, cos and regency (named in his honour). Other restaurants and retailers took up his clean green cause.

Collette Dinnigan

Born in New Zealand, Dinnigan started as a lingerie designer but found her customers were wearing her slips as dresses. She launched her own fashion label in Sydney in 1990, had a ready-to-wear parade in Paris in 1995 and now her finely beaded evening gowns are seen on red carpets around the world.

Gino di Santo

Arriving in 1952 from southern Italy, di Santo noticed a few gaps in our eating opportunities and proceeded to import pasta, sauces, wine, cappuccino machines and gelato makers. His Melbourne-based providore business, Enoteca Sileno, introduced Australians to extra virgin olive oil, balsamic vinegar, rice specially grown for risotto and fresh truffles.

Margaret Fulton

Starting as a demonstrator for the gas company in the 1950s, Fulton found she had a knack for explaining recipes to nervous homemakers. She created accessible but adventurous food sections for *Woman's Day* and *New Idea* and *The Margaret Fulton Cookbook*, published in 1968, sold 1.5 million copies. She gave confidence and inspiration to three generations of Australian cooks.

Akira Isogawa

Visiting Australia from Japan on a working holiday in 1986, Isogawa thought he might make a few bucks by reworking kimonos to suit Western bodies, and ended up staying and creating a new style of Japanese/Australian-global design.

Dare Jennings

A surfer who started a clothing line for teenagers called Mambo in 1984, Jennings encouraged artists to design shirts that might offend the occasional grandmother. 'We are really the only designers who reflect Australian culture in any kind of hip way,' he said. 'It's colourful, it's provocative, but it's not harbour bridges and bloody kangaroos. We like to take the piss out of people.' When he sold the business in 2001, it had become an international youth culture empire offering hats, pants, watches, bikes, posters and recordings. Other surf labels such as Quiksilver, Billabong and Rip Curl are just pale imitations.

Jenny Kee

Of Chinese, Italian and English background, Kee grew up at Sydney's Bondi Beach, experienced 'Swinging London' in the 1960s and in 1974 'started designing jumpers with this whole idea of having this real Australian flavour … hand knitting beautiful things and then putting these wonderful Australian images on them'. Then she began painting Australian animals, fish, flowers and birds and printing them on silk. Her company, Flamingo Park, found international fame when Diana Spencer wore her jumpers.

Graham Kennedy

Bursting onto Melbourne television in 1957, Kennedy smashed the 'Tonight Show' mould before it was even set. Nothing was sacred and all that mattered was getting a laugh, so he mocked his sponsors, his bosses and his audience. Appearing and disappearing in a variety of TV guises until his retirement in 1991, he embodied the larrikin we like to think lies in every Australian. He died in 2005.

Gilbert Lau

Appointed as host of Melbourne's Flower Drum restaurant in 1975, Lau surprised Australians with the notion that Chinese food could be much more than suburban takeaway. He showed how ancient dishes could be matched with modern wines, and how Cantonese cooking warranted as much analysis as French haute cuisine. He retired in 2004.

Eddie Mabo

A man of the Mer people of Murray Island in the Torres Strait, Mabo brought a case to the High Court which, in 1992, created the precedent for Aboriginal land rights. The court overturned the doctrine known as 'terra nullius', which said Australia had been 'empty' before white settlement, and ruled that Aboriginal and Torres Strait Islander peoples could claim ownership of their land if they proved continuous settlement since the 18th century. Mabo died six months before his victory was announced.

Hugh Mackay

A researcher into social attitudes since the 1970s, Mackay has a unique talent for assessing the mind and mood of the nation. Before him, Australians were rarely self-analytical. His newspaper columns and his 1993 book *Reinventing Australia* showed us how we were changing.

The Oz editors

In 1963 Richard Walsh, Richard Neville and Martin Sharp launched a satirical magazine called *Oz*. In 1964 they were each sentenced to six months gaol for obscenity (after publishing language and cartoons deemed offensive). The overturning of their conviction on appeal helped to break down the censorship imposed by Australian authorities on literature and art. Sharp and Neville founded a London edition of *Oz*, while Walsh moved into publishing.

Beppi Polese

Trained as a waiter in the great hotels of Italy, Polese reached Australia in 1952 and was shocked at how little pleasure we took in eating. He opened Beppi's in East Sydney in 1956 and set about converting Australians to weird ingredients such as mussels, calamari, eggplant, capsicum and artichokes. With his restaurant now in its fiftieth year, he's still there every lunchtime cajoling customers to 'just give this a try'.

Richard Smart

Trained in agricultural science at Sydney University in the 1960s, Smart became the world's most respected viticulturalist, with consulting rooms in Tasmania, Portugal, Peru and the United States. His book *Sunlight Into Wine* is an industry bible and he is credited with raising the drinking standards of 25 nations.

Working Dog

A loose collection of writers and actors based in Melbourne, Working Dog got together in the 1980s for the ABC TV comedy 'The D-Generation' then created the movies *The Castle* and *The Dish*; the TV shows 'Frontline', 'A River Somewhere', 'All Aussie Adventures', 'The Panel' and 'Thank God You're Here'; and the travel guides *Molvania*, *Phaic Tan* and *San Sombrero*. The members are Tom Gleisner, Santo Cilauro, Michael Hirsh, Jane Kennedy and Rob Sitch.

Mandawuy Yunupingu

A man of the Gumatj clan of north-east Arnhem Land, Yunupingu got a degree in education and became the first Aboriginal to be appointed as a school principal (at Yirrkala on the Gove Peninsula, Northern Territory), and in 1986 formed the rock band Yothu Yindi. Their song 'Treaty', using didgeridoo, bilma (clapsticks), electric guitars and drums, became a world hit in 1991 and the federal government named Yunupingu Australian of the Year in 1992.

Giuseppe Zuzza

Trained as a waiter in north-east Italy, Zuzza arrived in Australia in 1976 with ambition and a recipe. The recipe, borrowed from his friends at El Toula restaurant in the town of Treviso, involved coffee-soaked sponge, mascarpone, chocolate and Tia Maria liqueur. It was called 'tiramisu' (pick-me-up). Zuzza introduced it at Darcy's restaurant in Paddington, Sydney, and then at his own place, The Mixing Pot, in Glebe, Sydney. As other restaurateurs copied him, tiramisu spread across the country, and some form of it is now in every suburban bistro and supermarket. Its success symbolises the internationalisation of our tastes. If lamingtons represent the old Australia, the new Australia is tiramisu.

The sum of us

The average adult in this country has one breast and one testicle, and smokes four cigarettes a day. That is presumably who the politicians mean when they pontificate about what **the average Australian** wants, believes, knows to be true and won't stand for.

This fabulous creature emerges when you add up the number of testicles on this continent, or the number of breasts, or the number of cigarettes smoked in a day, and then divide by the number of people aged over 18 — a perfectly respectable way to reach an average, or mean. And you quickly understand why the Bureau of Statistics is wary about using such terms when it reports its findings, preferring to talk about the **median**: the point where half the population has more of the thing being measured and half has less than the thing being measured.

In mid 2005 the bureau set out to explain how rich we are in a report called 'Household Wealth and Wealth Distribution'. It revealed that the average household in Australia has assets (house, car, furniture, investments) of \$537 000 and liabilities of \$69 000 — a **net worth** of \$468 000. Those figures make us look pretty well off, evoking **a national snapshot** of smiling mum, dad, two kids and Holden in front of neat bungalow with a Hill's Hoist in the yard. Even without a white picket fence, it gives a reassuring impression of **a lucky country**.

But the Bureau warned against such an enthusiastic interpretation:

> While the mean household net worth of all households in Australia was \$468 000, the median (i.e. the mid-point when all households are ranked in ascending order of net worth) was substantially lower at \$295 000. This difference reflects the asymmetric **distribution of wealth** between households, where a relatively small proportion of households had relatively high net worth and a large number of households had relatively lower net worth.

What's happening is that the Packers, the Pratts, the Lowys and the Smorgons, with their mansions, planes, yachts and penthouses, are pulling up the average and making the rest of us look better off than we really are. In fact, half of Australia's households are worth less than \$295 000 — which does not suggest very comfortable living conditions at all. Only eight per cent have net worth above one million dollars, while 17 per cent of households (containing three million people) have net worth below $50 000.

The same problem came up when the Bureau looked at how well Australians are providing for their **retirements**. Divide the number of households with super into the total money in super funds and you get an average figure of $85 000. But 25 per cent of households have no super provision of any kind, and among those who do, half have superannuation assets under $35 000.

To indicate how **national wealth** has grown in recent years, the Bureau reported that between 1999 and 2004, prices for basic commodities grew 18 per cent, while our spending on recreation (entertainment, sport, holidays) grew 29 per cent, to a household average of $115 a week. But not all households are indulging themselves so furiously. Those in the bottom fifth of earnings spend only $43 a week on recreation.

So it's **all in the way you tell it**. You could say that 51 per cent of Australians have breasts, 49 per cent have testicles, 50 per cent have massively inadequate superannuation cover, 8 per cent are rich, 17 per cent are poor, 20 per cent don't have much fun, and 21 per cent smoke twenty cigarettes a day.

Now you know why you should approach with caution the information you're about to read. What follows is a portrait of a **representative Australian family**, based on a mixture of medians, means and most frequents. It's probable that more than half the families in Australia are a bit like this …

Meet Nicole and Michael Smith. He's 39, she's 37. They got married in 1995 after living together for a year, and they have two kids — Matthew, 11, and Emily, 8. Michael is 175 centimetres tall and weighs 82 kilograms but, if asked, would estimate he weighs 80 kilograms. Nicole is 161 centimetres tall and weighs 67 kilograms, but would say 65.

Michael earns $1100 a week in an administrative job, while Nicole earns $500 working three days a week in a shop. They are paying off a three-bedroom home with a small backyard in a suburb 25 kilometres from the sea. The house cost $500 000, and they still owe $113 000 on their mortgage, which they pay off at $110 a week. But they'll sell up and move to a new house within six years.

They still owe $2700 on their white Holden Commodore and right now they have a total credit card debt of $2000. Between them they lose $6 a week on gambling — a couple of scratchies at the newsagents and the occasional pull on the pokies at the pub when they go for dinner.

All four Smiths were born in Australia, but Nicole's parents were born in Britain. The Smiths wrote 'no religion' on their census form, while Michael's parents wrote Catholic and Nicole's parents wrote Anglican. Michael's father Ron died of a heart attack last year at the age of 69. Nicole's mother Margaret is recovering from breast cancer. They are starting to think Michael's mother Shirley may need to move to a nursing home.

Before she was married, Nicole had a four-week trip to London. Before he was married, Michael had a two-week trip to Thailand. Each year they drive for three-hours up or down the coast and take a five-day beach holiday. The family spent a week in New Zealand last year and is planning a trip to California next year.

The last book Michael read was *The Da Vinci Code*. Nicole buys *Women's Weekly* most months and passes it on to her mother. Each of the Smiths goes to the movies five times a year (together, mostly). Michael goes twice a year to football games. They rent a DVD every two weeks to watch on Saturday or Sunday night. In addition to the DVD player they installed last year, their home contains two TV sets, three mobile phones, a VCR, washing machine, microwave, fridge, dishwasher and computer, which is mainly used by Matthew.

They spend $25 a week on fast food and takeaway — McDonald's, pizza and Thai mostly — and eat out in a restaurant once a month, spending $80. Michael and Nicole spend $25 a week on alcohol, each drinking five glasses of wine (three white, two red) and two cans of beer. They each drink five cups of coffee a week, and two cups of tea.

The Smiths have had two encounters with crime in their lives: once when their car was stolen and once when they came home to discover a break-in, with their VCR and some cash missing.

Nicole takes the Pill. And as to how often they have sex, the information is unreliable. They would tell researchers it's about six times a month.

If you think you now know what the **majority of Australians** are like, think again. Families with children inhabit only 47 per cent of Australian homes. The nation's other homes contain couples without children, single-parent families, and people living alone (23 per cent and growing).

I described the Smiths because their structure is more common than any other configuration of household. But that claim to fame won't last much longer. The Bureau of Statistics made this revelation in 2004:

> 'Over the next 20 years, **couple households without children** are projected to become the most common of all family types, overtaking couple families with children in 2016 and comprising 42 per cent of families in 2021.'

Australia is changing fast, and *Who We Are* will be regularly revised to chronicle those changes.